SINGER

SEWING REFERENCE LIBRARY®

Sewing Update No. I

Cy DeCosse Incorporated
Minnetonka, Minnesota

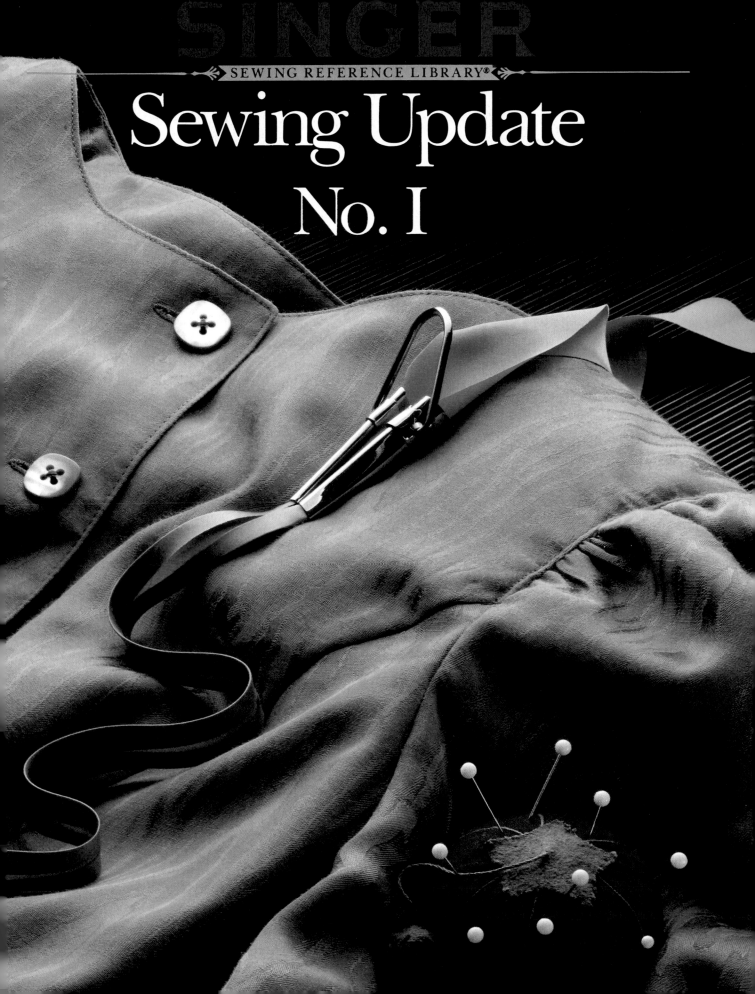

SINGER
SEWING REFERENCE LIBRARY®
Sewing Update No. I

Contents

Also available from the publisher: *Sewing Essentials, Sewing for the Home, Clothing Care & Repair, Sewing for Style, Sewing Specialty Fabrics, Sewing Activewear, The Perfect Fit, Timesaving Sewing, More Sewing for the Home, Tailoring*

Distributed by: Contemporary Books, Inc.
Chicago, Illinois

Library of Congress
Cataloging-in-Publication Data

Sewing Update No. 1

(Singer Sewing Reference Library)
1. Sewing. I. Title.
TT705.S475   1988   646.2   87-27284
ISBN 0-86573-237-X
ISBN 0-86573-238-8 (pbk.)

Credits

CY DE COSSE INCORPORATED
Chairman: Cy DeCosse
President: James B. Maus
Executive Vice President: William B. Jones

SEWING UPDATE NO. 1
Created by: The Editors of Cy DeCosse Incorporated, in cooperation with the Singer Education Department. Singer is a trademark of The Singer Company and is used under license.

Managing Editor: Reneé Dignan
Editorial Director: Carol Neumann
Art Director: Lisa Rosenthal
Editors: Bernice Maehren, Susan Meyers
Sample Supervisor: Rita Opseth
Technical Photo Director: Bridget Haugh
Sewing Staff: Phyllis Galbraith, Bridget Haugh, Carol Neumann, Barbara Caron, Kathy Davis Ellingson, Wendy Fedie, JoAnn Krause, Jules & Kaethe Kliot, Alice Lewis, Kathleen Pauser, Linda Powell, Marlys Ricdcscl, Valcric Ruthardt, Donna Salyers, Barbara Vik, Joanne Wawra
Photographers: Rex Irmen, Tony Kubat, John Lauenstein, Mark Macemon, Mette Nielsen
Production Manager: Jim Bindas
Assistant Production Managers: Julie Churchill, Jacquie Marx
Production Staff: Janice Cauley, Joe Fahey, Carol Ann Kevan, Yelena Konrardy, Christi Maybee, Dave Schelitzche, Linda Schloegel, Cathleen Shannon, Jennie Smith, Greg Wallace, Scott Winton, Nik Wogstad
Consultants: Doris Brashear, Charlene Burningham, Clotilde, Meta Hoge, Karen Kestel, Darlene Kinning, JoAnn Krause, Lynn Marquardt, Adele Martinek, Darlene Myers, Don Ringstrom, Donna Salyers, Jane Schenck, Cheryl Wanska, Nancy Zieman
Contributing Manufacturers: B. Blumenthal; Bionic Finger; Braid-Aid; Clotilde; Coats & Clark; Colwell General Inc.; Conso Products Co.; Crown Textile, Inc.; Dritz Corporation; Dyno Merchandise Corporation; Elna, Inc.; EZ International; Freudenberg, Pellon Division; JHB International; June Tailor, Inc.; Olfa; Quintessence; Rowenta, Inc.; The Singer Company; Stacy Industries, Inc.; Streamline Industries, Inc.; Swiss-Metrosene, Inc.; Thai Silks; Thumble, Inc.; Tootal American; Vin Max, Inc.; Wm. E. Wright Co.; YLI Corporation
Contributing Photographers: Calico Corners® Decorative Fabrics; Waverly, Division of F. Shumacher & Co.
Color Separations: Color Control
Printing: W. A. Krueger (0688)

Sewing for Today

Sewing Update No. 1 is dedicated to helping the sewer. Whether a beginner, an expert, or a sewer somewhere in between, you will find in this book current information on equipment, tools, notions, fabrics, color, and trends for wearable fashions, home fashions, and fiber art.

Treat this book as a sewer's consumer guide. Review fashion and decorating trends, techniques, equipment, and tools at your leisure. Select appropriate mail-order sources from our suggestions at the ends of articles. Check the Sources page at the end of the book for additional books, newsletters, magazines, and catalogs, as well as sources for consumer information. Use the book also to scheme and dream; much of the fun in any creative process is the planning and anticipation.

Wearable Fashions

Home sewers are looking for inspiration and information. In a survey we asked some of you what information you want for your sewing. You responded that you want up-to-the-minute information on styles and colors. We've included the techniques to achieve these styles, and we've provided ideas for accessories to add the final touch.

Home Fashions

Sewing for the home can be quick and simple. Knowing color and style trends will help you easily update your existing decor. Because time is at a premium, you want to sew only what will keep you, your family, and your home truly fashionable.

Equipment, Tools & Notions

The sewer also wants timely information on the latest in sewing machines, sergers, pressing equipment, tools, and notions. Keeping pace with changing methods and new technology can help make the most of sewing time.

In our high-tech world, major equipment items are continually evolving. Just as computers, VCRs, and compact disc players were unheard of a few years ago, especially for the home user, the same is true for the latest developments in sewing machines. Computer technology has made its impact on the sewing machine industry, and new features are constantly appearing. Within the last eight years, sergers have moved from industry to the home and revolutionized home sewing. The home sewer can now duplicate industry techniques and, most important, speed up the sewing process.

The body of knowledge has doubled since World War I — or maybe it only seems that way because of the rapid expansion of mass communications. Nowhere is this change more evident than in the proliferation of catalogs. We have gathered the best catalog sources and included their addresses for your convenience. It is important to read catalogs because stores carry only what sells. Some notions with limited appeal can be best carried by mail-order sources, where large inventories are not necessary.

This book will review the newest of the new, discuss the advantages and disadvantages of products, and, in some cases, give opinions on their usefulness. Please keep in mind that what works for one may not work for another, and use opinions only as a guide.

Fiber Art

We haven't forgotten those sewers who are interested in fiber art. We have included traditional home crafts that have transcended the crafty connotation and become true art in design, quality, and technique.

This section is designed to whet your appetite. Not all articles supply detailed instructions. Instead, we've provided enough information for you to decide whether the project suits your creative urge.

For most crafts, printed information is available in books and magazines or through your local retailers. You may also find local classes through stores, community education, extension agencies, junior colleges, vocational schools, universities, and colleges.

Our Writers

All our writers are in a position to know about sewing, either through their daily work or their ability to find those who do know. Most earn a living by dealing with sewing on a daily basis: they teach, write, consult, design, sell, experiment, and learn. Some are freelance writers with an uncanny ability to seek out the very best sources of information.

We are dedicated to bringing the home sewer up-to-date information that will ensure sewing successes, offer inspiration, and give sewing the savvy, chic image it deserves. *Sewing Update No. 1* provides decision-making information for all levels of sewing experience. It also educates the consumer that sewing today is easier and quicker than ever.

Sew Smart

Sewing: A Creative Outlet

by JoAnn Krause

Within each of us lies the desire to create something from nothing — something unique and original. For many, sewing fulfills this basic creative need. It's not just relaxing and enjoyable; the process of transforming a piece of cloth into a unique garment is exciting.

It's time to reevaluate your attitude toward sewing. Rethink your schedule, and give yourself enough time to enjoy being creative. Memorize construction sequence. Cut out several garments at once. Use the most efficient and timesaving tools. Make your motto "Sew it today: wear it today!"

The most important tools are the basic patterns: blouse, jacket, skirt, and pants. Acquire a set of basic patterns with interchangeable parts, such as pockets, cuffs, collars, and sleeves, that you can use year after year. Familiarity with a pattern eliminates reading instructions and prefitting. In a short time you will become comfortable with your patterns and their interchangeable parts and will begin to develop a pattern wardrobe that is uniquely you. Multi-sized patterns allow you to use several sizes for one garment. Compare pattern measurements with a favorite ready-to-wear garment to save time in fitting.

A scrapbook of sketches, fashion notes, and pictures of your favorite designer garments will be invaluable when you redesign your basic patterns. Basic patterns are easily updated with the use of current fabrics that you see in ready-to-wear.

The main equipment that you need is a good-quality conventional sewing machine that does zigzag stitching. A serger is the second most important purchase when you decide to expand. To produce an original, professional designer garment, use edgestitching, topstitching, and twin-needle stitching.

To add variety to fabric shopping, consider fabric warehouses and drapery and linen departments. Tapestries are ideal for jackets and vests. Doilies, bread basket liners, and napkins make beautiful, unique collars and blouse inserts. Recycle used sweaters into matching hat, mittens, and leg warmers. Flaws in fabrics sometimes force us to be creative. For example, you could add an appliqué or strip of material to cover the flaw.

You can create your own designer fabric by piecing together different fabrics such as sweater knits and wovens, lace and fabric to give the look of insertion, and narrow lace trims to create lace yardage. Tuck, pleat, or twin-needle stitch the fabric to form an interesting surface design. Cut out the pattern after completing your designer fabric.

Refashion sweaters, coats, and trims into a totally new garment through the use of overlays. Remove sweater ribbing to use as cuffs or bands with fleece and woven fabrics. You'll get a designer look at a fraction of the cost.

To complete your wardrobe, use fabric remnants to make handbags, eyeglass cases, cosmetic cases, hats, belts, bows, accent roses, and jabots. This is a perfect chance to let your imagination go wild. You can do so much with so little, with the bonus of using your creative gift.

JoAnn Krause has been a sewing specialist, motivational instructor, and TV personality for twenty years. She has written JK Originals *instruction manuals, patterns, and videos.*

Fabric Shopping by Mail

by Barbara Weiland O'Connell

Your local fabric store can't possibly stock everything you'd love to sew, but with a little armchair sleuthing, you can have it all — from feather boas and couture silks to hard-to-find sweater knits, from the mundane to the exotic and everything in between. Thanks to the popularity of mail-order shopping over the last decade, fabric retailers and wholesalers have joined the bandwagon, offering improved shop-at-home services to fabric aficionados.

One of the biggest advantages of armchair fabric shopping is a more comprehensive selection right at your fingertips. In addition, it can eliminate frustration and save the time and transportation costs that come with shopping at all the local fabric stores.

On the minus side, you often have only a small swatch to examine, or sometimes only a photograph of a swatch. That makes it difficult to determine how the fabric feels and drapes, so you must rely on previous knowledge of a similar fabric and a bit of guesswork. Of course, there's also the wait once you've placed your order. If you're in a rush for a specific fabric, you can usually request, and pay for, overnight or second-day air service.

Fabric mail-order firms offer a variety of services, including personalized swatching when you're looking for something special. Some charge for this service, and some don't. Most send out swatch sets, ranging from just a few to hundreds of fabric samples of their current offerings. These may be accompanied by periodic sales notices and fashion reports.

Some of the most helpful mail-order services compile swatches into coordinated groupings to assist with wardrobe planning, and at least one source supplies color notations corresponding to seasonal color analysis. Most will apply the cost of swatch sets to your initial purchase. Some supply a gift certificate to offset the price. Either way, it's your responsibility to ask for the refund or return the certificate with your order.

A word to the wise: with more suppliers joining the ranks of mail-order fabric services, you could spend a small fortune on swatch sets and annual memberships. So before you send off your check, read the descriptive literature carefully to make sure the service carries the kinds of fabrics you normally like to sew and wear.

Ordering Guidelines

Fill out the order form, printing clearly. Supply your daytime phone number so the company can reach you easily if there are any questions about your order.

If you're charging your order, be sure to include the complete charge card number, the expiration date, and the exact way your name appears on the credit card. You must also use your legal signature in the space provided to authorize the company to charge to your card.

If you will accept substitutions in case the fabric is out of stock, give clear descriptions, including catalog number, page number, and color.

If possible, send the swatch or a portion of the swatch of the fabric you're ordering.

If you're searching for something specific, call or write selected sources with a complete description of the fabric. If possible, send color samples for matching purposes. Mail-order sources affiliated with, or divisions of, large full-service fabric stores will naturally have more diversified selections to offer.

Be sure to read the information on the order form about returns and product guarantees. It is best not to buy from a source who won't accept returns.

If ordering by phone, fill out the order form to use as a reference when talking with the order clerk and to verify your order.

Keep all paperwork until you have received your order and are satisfied. If you have questions about the dollar transaction, you cannot be charged interest until the matter has been cleared to your satisfaction.

When you receive your order, inspect it thoroughly to check color and yardage. Also check for obvious flaws, and if the merchandise is not satisfactory, make arrangements immediately to return it for credit or replacement.

Barbara Weiland O'Connell is a nationally known sewing expert, columnist, and author. Her most recent book is Clothes Sense: Straight Talk about Wardrobe Planning, *co-authored with Leslie Wood.*

Guide to Fabric Alternatives

Company	Description	Address
Altra Inc.	Kits and fabrics for skiwear and crafts.	100 E. Washington St., New Richmond, IN 47967; (800) 443-8714
Bridals International	Special collection of imported laces and fabrics plus design ideas.	45 Albany St., Cazenovia, NY 13035
Britex-by-Mail	Swatching available. Watch for monthly specials advertised in fashion and sewing magazines.	146 Geary St., San Francisco, CA 94108
Classic Cloth	For the best selection of boiled wool plus hand-picked challis to match; Liberty of London cottons.	2508-D McMullen Booth Rd., Clearwater, FL 34621
Fabric Gallery	Four swatch mailings a year for nominal fee. Imported and domestic silks, wools, cottons, better blends, and synthetics.	146 W. Grand River, Williamston, MI 48895
Fabric Wholesalers, Inc.	Only for small manufacturers or fabric-based businesses. Send for price list and coupon.	Box 20235, Portland, OR 97220
Fabrics by Phone	Swatching service of fabrics for home decorating. Also offers custom-made service for draperies, bedspreads, and accessories.	Box 309, Walnut Bottom, PA 17266; (800) 233-7012, or (800) 692-7345 in Pennsylvania
Fabrics in Vogue	Six swatch mailings for annual membership fee. Offers fabrics the same as, or similar to, those featured in *Vogue Patterns* magazine.	Suite 303 East, 200 Park Avenue, New York, NY 10166
G Street Fabrics	Sample charts of basics plus Ultrasuede® and Facile®. Swatching available. Call or write for current listing of sample sets and prices.	11854 Rockville Pike, Rockville, MD 20852
The Green Pepper, Inc.	Catalog of activewear fabrics, including water repellent fabrics, insulated batting, and nylon and polypropylene/Lycra® blend knits.	941 Olive St., Eugene, OR 97401
Imaginations	Subscription brings four seasonal swatched catalogs of designer fabrics. Swatches are coded for color analysis systems.	32 Concord St., Framingham, MA 01701; (800) 343-6953
Iowa Pigskin Sales Co.	Suede and smooth, full-grain pigskin in a range of colors. Sample set fee refunded with order.	Box 115, Clive, IA 50053
Jehlor Fantasy Fabrics	Catalog of specialty fabrics, including sequined and metallic yardage, stretch fabrics, plus beads, sequins, jewels, and fantasy trims.	730 Andover Park West, Seattle, WA 98188
Kieffers Lingerie Fabrics & Supplies	Free catalog of lingerie and activewear fabrics, including lace trims and elastics.	1625 Hennepin Ave., Minneapolis, MN 55403
Left Bank Fabric Co. by Mail	Membership fee refundable over the year's purchases. Unlimited personal swatching. Fine imports and designer fabrics.	8354 W. 3rd St., Los Angeles, CA 90048
Patty's Pincushion, Inc.	Offers personalized service for planning wedding gowns. Send sketch or picture of gown and veil ideas; for a small fee, you will receive swatches of fabrics, linings, lace, and millinery supplies. Prices and estimated yardage included.	At Grande Affaires, 710 Smithfield St., Pittsburgh, PA 15219
The Rain Shed	Outdoor fabric, patterns, notions. Definitions of terms, fabrics, insulations, tools, and notions.	707 NW 11th St., Corvallis, OR 97330
Seventh Avenue Designer Fabric Club	Four coordinated fabric selections, illustrated catalogs, and special sales on designer fabrics.	Suite 900, 701 Seventh Ave., New York, NY 10036
Thai Silks	Yearly fabric club membership plus complete swatch sets for a fee applicable to purchase.	252 State St., Los Altos, CA 94022; (800) 722-SILK, or (800) 221-SILK in California
Utex Trading	Everything silk from thread and yarn to couture prints. Deposit required. SASE for details.	Suite 5, 710 Ninth St., Niagara Falls, NY 14301

Patterns for Every Occasion

by Anne Marie Soto

Whether you're searching for the perfect business suit, the wedding dress of your dreams, a re-creation of a sixteenth century ballgown, or a Japanese chabaori jacket, there's a pattern for you — if you only know where to look.

Pattern companies, large and small, offer the home sewer a wonderful assortment of designs; however, it's impractical for one fabric store to carry every pattern from every manufacturer. To find specialty patterns or designs from smaller manufacturers, you may need to do some armchair shopping.

The major pattern companies are those that offer a full range of styles, from daytime to evening wear, in a variety of sizes. They produce the large, heavy monthly or seasonal catalogs that you find in the fabric stores. Each catalog contains a carefully indexed assortment of several hundred styles. It's great fun to go to the fabric store and pore over all these pages, but it's not necessary to do that every time you want a new pattern. There are at-home alternatives.

The following information will help you discover a world of pattern shopping available without your having to leave the comfort of your own living room.

Anne Marie Soto, nationally known expert in the field of fashion sewing, is the author of numerous articles and publications, including Vogue's Sewing for Your Children.

Guide to Alternative Pattern Shopping

Pattern	Description	Address	Price
Bridal Elegance®	Interchangeable bodice, sleeve, skirt patterns for gowns	Bridal Elegance, 1176 Northport Dr., Columbus, OH 43220	Free brochure
Burda	Mini-catalog; German-based company	Burda Patterns, Box 2517, Smyrna, GA 30081	SASE
Butterick®	*The Butterick Home Catalog*	The Butterick Pattern Co., Box 1552, Altoona, PA 16603	$7 a year
Coat Craze	Multi-sized outerwear, skiwear	Durfee's Coats, Box 314, Shelley, ID 83274	Free brochure
Colten Creations	Patterns for expectant and nursing mothers	Colten Creations, Dept. SU1, Potters 54 Burk Dr., Silver Bay, MN 55614	Free brochure
Fashion Blueprints®	Ethnic designs with special craft focus	Fashion Blueprints, 2191 Blossom Valley Dr., San Jose, CA 95124	$1 for catalog
Folkwear®	Cultural or historical designs; includes men's, children's	Folkwear, Box 3859, San Rafael, CA 94912	$1 for catalog
Great Fit Patterns™	Large size women's patterns, sizes 38 to 60	Great Fit Patterns, 221 SE 197th Ave., Portland, OR 97233	$1 for catalog
Green Pepper	Outerwear, aerobic, and bicycling patterns; fabric and notions	The Green Pepper, Inc., 941 Olive St., Eugene, OR 97401	$1 for catalog
Jean Hardy	Classic and western attire	Jean Hardy Pattern Co., 2151 La Cuesta Dr., Santa Ana, CA 92705	$1 for catalog
KidSew®	Patterns designed to teach preteens to sew	KidSew, Box 20627, Columbus, OH 43220	Free brochure
Kwik-Sew®	*Kwik-Sew Home Catalog*	Kwik-Sew, 3000 Washington Ave. N., Minneapolis, MN 55411	$3
Lord Lass	Maternity and nursing patterns for sportswear and evening wear	Lord Lass, Box 26032, Albuquerque, NM 87125	$2 for catalog, refundable
McCall's	*McCall's Patterns* magazine	McCall's Patterns Magazine, Box 2022, Mahopac, NY 10541	$8.50 a year
Old World Sewing Pattern Company	Historical re-creations of 19th century fashions	Old World Sewing Pattern Co., Rte. 2, Box 103, Cold Spring, MN 57320	$1 for catalog
Patterns Pacifica/Pauloa	Contemporary designs inspired by the tropics, Orient, and Hawaii	Pattern People, Dept. AMS, Box 11254, Honolulu, HI 96828	$1 for catalog
Pineapple Appeal®	Garments and small projects for teens to sew	Pineapple Appeal, 538 Maple Dr., Box 197, Owatonna, MN 55060	Free catalog
Raindrops & Roses	Maternity and nursing patterns for working mothers	Raindrops & Roses, Box 14615, Portland, OR 97214	$1 for catalog
The Rain Shed	Sportswear patterns, notions, fabric	The Rain Shed, 707 NW 11th St., Corvallis, OR 97330	Free catalog
Simplicity®	*Simplicity* magazine	Simplicity, 200 Madison Ave., New York, NY 10016	$6 for three issues a year
Stretch & Sew®	Mini-catalog available through local retailer	Stretch & Sew Inc., Box 185, Eugene, OR 97440; (800) 547-7717	
Style®	Mini-catalog, European influence; newest addition to U.S. market	Style Patterns, 200 Madison Ave., New York, NY 10016	Free
Sunrise Designs®	Preemie, infant, toddler, and children's patterns	Sunrise Industries, Box 277, Orem, UT 84057	Free catalog
Vogue®	*Vogue Patterns* magazine; Vogue Patterns Portfolio	Vogue Patterns, Box 549, Altoona, PA 16603	$11.95 a year $19.95 a year

The Importance of Quality
by Clotilde

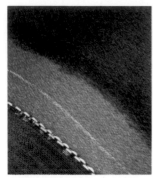

The better the ingredients, the better the result. Your mother told you this about baking a cake, but did she apply it to sewing as well? Too often you may skimp on sewing essentials: thread, interfacing, scissors, as well as fabric. You say you're sewing to save money? But what will be the result? Probably the bargain basement look instead of a designer look. Think instead that you're sewing to have more clothes of better fabric and construction.

Don't settle for a so-so color, last year's hem length, or a too-short waistline. Sew something that is one of a kind, not a carbon copy of hundreds of other dresses. Whether sewing a sweatshirt, unlined jacket, or prom dress, you'll have the color, style, and fit you want.

Sew with the best fabric and interfacing you can afford. Sewing time is the same whether they are from the bargain or couture fabric table. Interfacing that is three yards for $1 and thread that costs five spools for $1 are all right for Halloween costumes, but don't waste time or money using them in clothes to wear again and again.

Price alone does not determine good or poor fabric. No matter how much you read about different fibers, from cotton voile to wool challis, your fingers must tell the difference. Fingers can learn the difference between antique porcelain and new china by feeling and comparing textures, densities, and glazes. So,

too, they can become educated to feel poor-quality fabrics with excess sizing that washes out in the first laundering. Crumple fabric to see whether wrinkles fall out. Educated fingers can find that treasure on the remnant table; mine do, and so can yours.

Read fiber content labels. A 65/35 cotton/polyester blend gives no-iron, wrinkle-free properties; 100 percent cotton is more comfortable but will require ironing. There are many weights of silk: crisp, heavy, soft, and thin. Also ask questions. What are the cleaning instructions? Is there a return policy on fabric that changes drastically after one washing?

Quality tools are important, too. Sharp shears cut easily and accurately. Smooth, sharp pins and machine needles don't leave holes and snags. (Always stitch across a scrap of fabric first to be sure the needle has no burrs.) A trouble-free sewing machine is a must and makes you want to sew. Nothing is more frustrating than continually adjusting tension. It's enough to make you give up sewing!

Other essentials are an iron that gives lots of steam and doesn't drip, a well-padded ironing board, and plenty of light. Good lighting is the best investment you can make for good sewing and for your eyes. Drafting lamps give intense light where needed and are available in art supply and sewing machine stores.

Quality fabric, tools, and workmanship result in a special garment. You'll be proud to say, "I made it."

Clotilde is a nationally recognized sewing authority, author, lecturer, and TV host. She founded her mail-order notions company, Clotilde, Inc., in 1972.

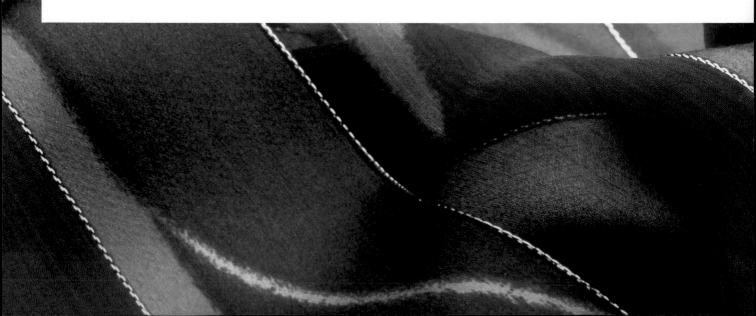

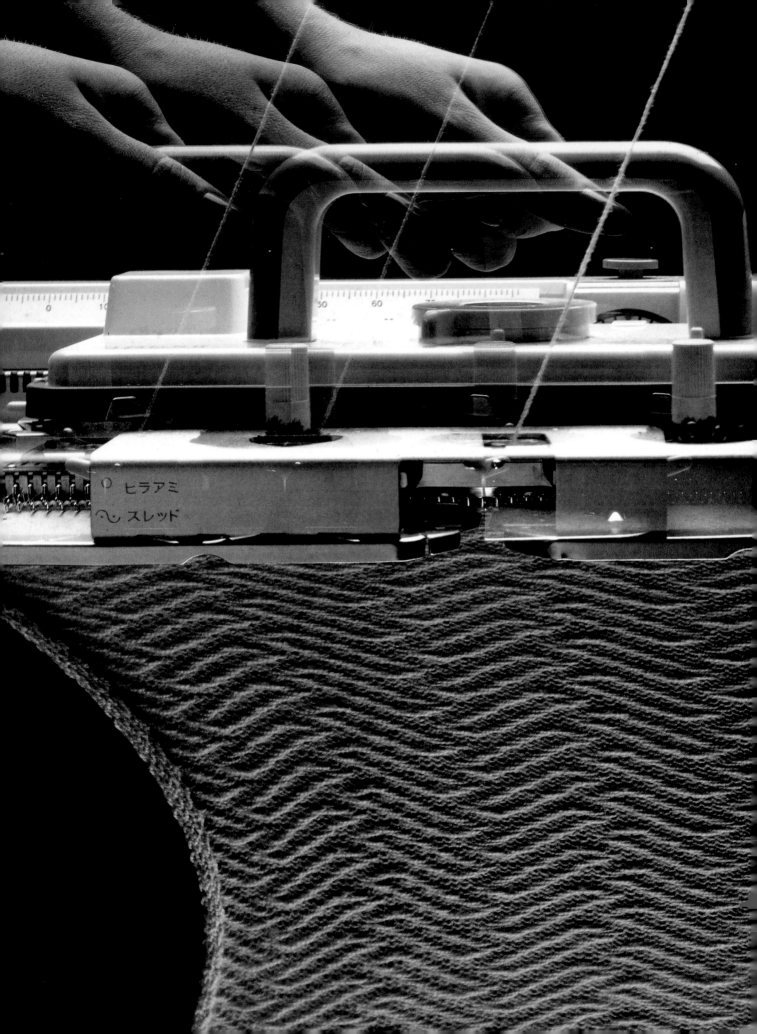

Equipment, Tools & Notions

So You Want to Buy a Sewing Machine

by Carol Neumann

Some old sewing machines never die; they are just recycled to daughters and granddaughters, college students, beginning sewers, and newlyweds. And like a good soldier, they continue to serve.

Unlike many consumer items, sewing machines do not have built-in obsolescence. Nor do they self-destruct three days after the warranty expires. All sewing machine manufacturers take pride in quality material and workmanship.

Many people are perfectly satisfied with a twenty or thirty-year-old machine. Some even retain an old treadle machine and swear by its reliability and stitch quality. To be perfectly honest, all you need to sew is a machine that produces a quality straight stitch and zigzag stitch on a variety of fabrics. However, certain new sewing machine features speed up sewing and contribute to sewing ease, accuracy, and fun. Also, newly developed fabrics may be difficult to sew on older machines produced before these fabrics were available. For this reason, you may wish to upgrade your sewing machine and either retire the "old soldier" from active-duty status to standby reserve or recycle it.

Whether upgrading your machine or purchasing your first machine, you will be faced with some difficult choices and perplexing decisions. In an effort to simplify the bewildering complexities involved in shopping, let's reduce the considerations to needs, features, quality, and price.

Just a word of advice: there will be no one machine that is all things to all sewers. Carefully evaluate your needs, standards of quality, machine features, and budget. Remember, all of these are interrelated, but only you can make the final decision. The sewing machine you choose may even be quite different from the one selected by another sewer with similar needs.

Needs & Features

Durability and dependability should be at the top of your list, but they are difficult to evaluate until the machine has been in continued use. To ensure quality, buy from a reputable dealer, select a known brand, and ask opinions of sewing friends.

Type and amount of sewing will help you decide on features for your machine. Certain features are basic necessities, whereas others are luxurious extras that may not be used or may be used infrequently. Compare basics and extras. Decide which are important for your sewing needs. If a machine will be used only for mending, decorative stitches will not be necessary. One of the frustrations of purchasing any consumer item is that to get those features you want most, you may have to purchase features you don't want. For example, most people want a machine that produces a quality buttonhole with ease, but an automatic buttonholer may be available only on a top-of-the-line machine. Consequently, you may end up buying features you have no intention of using. You could turn this into an advantage by considering the extra features as an investment in developing your sewing skills. Experiment with various stitches to determine how you can use them in your sewing.

Quality & Price

The finished product is only as good as the tools with which it is made. Many sewers think that the lack of sewing success is due to their technique when it may be due to the quality of the machine. Broken needles and thread, poor tension, and wavy stitching lines are often blamed on the operator when the machine may be at fault.

Prices range from about $99 to $1800. The lower end of the scale usually offers straight stitches and zigzag stitches, and may be all you need. Additional dollars spent for sewing machines are usually for convenience features. Whatever the price of the sewing machine, thoroughly test for quality stitches; don't sacrifice here!

Consumer Guide® recommends the mid-price range as the most practical for the average home sewer. The American Home Sewing Association makes a similar recommendation: Don't pay for more features than you will use, but don't economize by selecting a machine that will fall short of your expectations a year from now. Probably the best advice is to buy the best quality you can afford. Watch for sales. It is a rare occasion when you find it impossible to buy at sale price. Bargain with price and trade-ins. The worst that can happen is a refusal.

Basic Machine Features

Easy threading and bobbin winding.

Easy stitch selection, and width and length selection.

Sews off edge of fabric without jamming.

Variety of utility stitches to join seams, overcast edges, topstitch, hem, sew over elastic, sew stretch fabrics, and darn.

Variety of attachments, such as blind hem foot, zipper foot, button foot, buttonhole attachment.

Needle plate with seam guide markings.

Variable speed control for stitching accuracy.

Easy to clean, limited amount of oiling.

Instruction book you can understand.

Ability to sew from thick to thin, or vice versa, without skipping stitches.

Easily accessible attachment storage.

Free arm capability.

Extra Machine Features

Bobbin with large holding capacity, eliminating frequent rewinding; wind-in-place bobbin.

Limited amount of readjustment when changing stitches.

Stitch memory for self-repeating stitch pattern.

Knobs, controls, and lighting designed for the visually or physically disabled person.

Automatic buttonholer that measures length of buttonhole to ensure consistent buttonhole size.

Left/center/right needle position control.

Automatic needle threader for easy threading.

Electronic foot control that allows slow stitching without limiting piercing power of needle.

"Talking" machine with bleeps that act as reminders.

Even feeding capability.

A large variety of decorative stitches.

Up and down needle positioning.

Stitches & Other Features

The following utility stitches should be mandatory on any machine purchased in 1988: straight, zigzag, 3-step zigzag, blind hem, and a darning/mending stitch that can be adjusted to various lengths and widths. Look for adjustable widths; the wider widths of 6 to 8 mm are nice for appliqué and machine embroidery. These stitches will meet the total needs of 80 percent of all sewers.

A stretch stitch is a nice extra. However, the built-in straight stretch stitch is slow, uses too much thread, and is impossible to rip out. It is best used for reinforcement. A zigzag stitch may also be used on any stretch fabric.

Needle up/down selector allows you to decide where the needle will be when you stop stitching. In the up position, the machine stops with the needle in the highest take-up position. The stitch cycle has been completed, and the needle will not unthread when stitching is resumed. In the down position, the machine stops with the needle in the fabric, allowing you to make fabric adjustments without losing your place in the fabric. This feature is important for topstitching and applying elastic.

Needle positions are left, center, and right. These positions are extremely helpful for topstitching and machine embroidery. For example, position the needle to the right for edgestitching. The edge of the presser foot is used as a stitching guide, and the stitches are close to the fabric edge.

Wind-in-place bobbin allows winding of bobbin without removing it from the bobbin case.

Bobbin stop means the machine will automatically stop when the bobbin is full. Some bobbins have lines indicating full, so the operator can stop the machine.

Rotary shuttle rotates a full 360°. It is virtually jam-proof, allowing you to sew off the edge of the fabric for decorative stitches and machine lacemaking.

Oscillating shuttle swings back and forth like a pendulum. It may be somewhat easier to jam than the rotary shuttle. However, it is readily available to manufacturers, so it is usually found on lower-priced models. If well made, the oscillating shuttle should perform as well as the rotary shuttle.

Buttonholers may be 2-step, 4-step, or automatic. The 2-step and 4-step refer to the number of adjustments the operator makes. No pivoting of fabric is necessary. Automatic buttonholer attachments determine buttonhole length by measuring the button, or the length is set by the sewer.

Electronic machines are, technically, any machine with a form of electronic circuitry. The most common electronic element is the speed control, which allows the operator to sew fabric of any weight and to sew over many seam allowance layers when sewing jean hems, for example, without losing speed or control. This feature may be an advantage when you perform difficult techniques or sew on difficult fabrics. It also allows slow stitching without limiting the piercing power of the needle. Other mechanical functions may be controlled electronically. The touch of a button transmits an electrical current to perform a task such as moving the needle up or down. Without the electronic switch, the handwheel would need to be rotated mechanically to position the needle.

Computerized machines are electronic machines with a microcomputer. They are at the top of the line in features and price. They have the ability to memorize, store, and retrieve data. The computer makes the sewing machine very easy to operate. Stitch selection is a one-button operation. The computerized machine will automatically select the most appropriate stitch length, width, and tension. Some machines are programmed to select stitches according to the fabric being used and the type of sewing, and they even tell the sewer the proper presser foot to use. Computerized machines also allow the sewer to string a series of stitch patterns together, reverse images, produce mirror images, or double the length of a stitch pattern. Look for the ability to enlarge designs, a nice feature if you want to embroider logos. Look for overrides for automatic selections to allow for greater versatility. Particularly important is the ability to override stitch length, width, and tension selections.

Computerized machines memorize buttonhole length and repeat as often as necessary. This is an excellent feature since consistent buttonholes are a mark of quality sewing. Most automatic buttonholers memorize length by counting stitches. As a result, each side of the buttonhole bar will have an equal number of stitches. However, fabric irregularities may cause stitches to pile up and the buttonhole will be too short. Machines that measure length will repeat that length no matter how many stitches are needed, and the buttonholes will all be equal in size.

As with all computers, any program will be lost when the machine is turned off unless a backup power source is provided. Some machines will store data up to twenty-four hours after the machine is turned off. Losing a program will be a problem only if an original stitch sequence has been developed by the sewer.

Magnetic pin cushions used near the machine should not cause a problem for the computer, but avoid stick-on magnetic pin catchers that exert a constant magnetic pull.

Free arm is a convenience for mending and sewing tubular seams, such as armholes. The free arm is available on new models.

Self-lubricating means that oil is embedded in the machine's metal parts, eliminating the need for messy oiling.

Snap-on presser feet save time and are available on new models.

High-lift presser bar permits easy placement of thick seams and fabrics under the presser foot.

Universal pressure system automatically adjusts to various fabric thicknesses and weights. Depending on the kind of sewing, an override may be useful.

Dual feed capability simplifies sewing slippery fabrics, matching plaids and stripes, and quilting.

Here are some additional items to examine when shopping:

- A combination sewing machine/serger that is on a turntable. One side is a conventional sewing machine; the other is a 2-thread serger.

- A knee lifter to raise and lower the presser foot for continuous hands-on control of the fabric.

- Additional programs to expand the number of stitches on a computerized machine.

- The ability to sew sideways. This is a good idea for mending hard-to-reach areas such as knees.

- An accessory that allows the machine to sew in circles. This feature is excellent for embellishing items such as placemats, collars, and baby bibs.

Machine features include snap-on presser foot, high-lift presser bar, up/down needle positioning, and light source at needle.

- Embroidery attachment that expands the machine's embroidery capabilities to include programmed motifs and monograms.

Shopping for a Sewing Machine

When comparative shopping, look at a minimum of three sewing machines. Highlight the features that are important to you. Ask the dealer to demonstrate the machine, making sure the features you are interested in are explained. Be sure to examine the sewing machine manual. It should provide clear, concise instructions.

Allow yourself plenty of time, and try not to shop during peak customer hours. Don't overdo it by trying to test all your choices in one day. It will only confuse you. When you have examined all your choices, take some time to evaluate all you have learned and to make a decision. Talk with your sewing friends about their likes and dislikes concerning their own machines.

A dealer demonstration should include basic machine operations:

- Starting the machine without turning the handwheel by hand.

- Adjusting the top tension.

- Setting the stitch length regulator.

- Setting the needle bar in the left, center, and right positions on a zigzag machine.

- Sewing, using all functions that are available on the machine.

- Installing a double needle and top-threading the machine.

- Sewing a buttonhole.

- Sewing on a button.

Testing the Machine

Now you are ready for hands-on testing, which requires some prior preparation at home; you will need to make a test patch for each machine you test. Dealers sometimes provide a heavily starched, coarsely woven test patch. This patch is not adequate for successfully testing a machine's capabilities, because it is not typical of the fabric that you usually sew.

Cut two samples 4" by 4" (10 by 10 cm) and 4" by 5" (10 by 12.5 cm) of the following fabric types: light, medium, and heavyweight woven; light and medium-weight knits; stretch knit (swimwear); and as many novelty fabrics (such as sweater knit, leather, fake fur, Ultrasuede®, and terry cloth) as you might possibly sew. You will also need several 2" (5 cm) squares of interfacing.

Make rows of stitches the entire length of the patch to test stitch quality and to see how the machine deals with various fabric weights and multiple thicknesses. Test edge finishing stitches on the single layer of the patch. Place a square of interfacing between swatches of the patch; make buttonholes over these interfaced areas on both woven and knitted fabric swatches.

Arrange the test patch swatches, right side to wrong side, with the smaller swatch on top and one side aligned. Overlap each set of swatches by ½" (1.3 cm), and baste together by machine or with glue stick.

When you stitch on the test patch, evaluate the stitch quality by examining the straightness of the stitch line, its consistency, and tension. Check for stitch straightness by stitching straight lines at various stitch lengths. Set the stitch length at 0, position the fabric, and lower the presser foot. Turn the handwheel by hand to see whether the needle stitches in the same hole on each downstroke of the needle. Another good check for stitch quality is on buttonholes. A poorly stitched buttonhole ruins an otherwise finely made garment. Consistent stitches remain uniform in length through varying fabric types, weights, and thicknesses.

Although a size 14 (90) needle will work on the test patch, you may wish to change needle size for the light and heavy fabrics, and use a ballpoint needle for swimwear.

With correct tension, the top and bobbin thread interlock between the double fabric layers or within the fabric itself on the single layer. Lightweight single layers of fabric should show minimal loops on the right and wrong sides. Machines with self-adjusting tensions automatically adjust according to the specific stitch, length, and width; on these machines the tension should not require manual adjustment unless dealing with extremes in fabric weight.

Ask if the dealer provides classes on the use of the machine. Whether you spend $100 or $1000, you will get the most from your investment if you can use the machine to its maximum. The memory of a demonstration is never as long lasting as hands-on experience.

Carol Neumann is a staff member of the Singer Sewing Reference Library with experience in sewing, education, and retail fabric sales.

24

Sewing Machine Maintenance

by Claire Shaeffer

Your sewing machine is your most important piece of equipment. With a regular home maintenance program, a quality machine will give you years of sewing pleasure long after the warranty expires.

The more you sew, the more often you should clean your machine. In fact, you can't keep your machine too clean. The same applies to a serger if you have one. Sewing machines today accumulate more lint and dust than older models, perhaps because the needle hole is larger and many materials — synthetic fabrics, embroidery threads, polyester fleece, and needlepunch insulation — have more lint and fuzz.

If you haven't reviewed your sewing machine manual lately, you should familiarize yourself with your machine, its features, and requirements. Some machines need to be lubricated as well as oiled; some are self-oiling.

A good plan is to schedule a routine cleaning at the end of each sewing day. But you should also learn to recognize the sounds that indicate an accumulation of lint between the feed dogs and needle plate so that you'll know if your machine needs cleaning more often.

To clean the machine, remove the bobbin case, then the needle plate, even if it must be unscrewed. Next, using a brush, remove large particles of lint and dust from around the feed dogs and shuttle. Blow out any remaining dust with compressed air or a hair dryer set at cool temperature. Use a good-quality sewing machine oil, and oil sparingly where indicated in the manual. Occasionally clean between the tension discs with a piece of soft, lint-free fabric and check the needle plate and hook for rough places, which may require professional attention.

You can solve many sewing machine problems easily by reviewing the suggestions in your sewing machine manual, cleaning the machine, rethreading it, and changing the needle. If you have a major problem, take the machine and a sample of the fabric that you

are sewing to your dealer. Your machine should be checked by a factory-trained professional just before the warranty expires and again every two years, whether it needs it or not.

To prevent rust and corrosion, avoid airtight plastic dust covers and exposure to open windows. If your machine will be stored for extended periods, clean and oil it before putting it away and again when you take it out. If possible, avoid storing it in a garage, attic, basement, or any other place that gets very hot, very cold, or damp.

Claire Shaeffer has taught garment construction and fashion design in college and adult programs. She is the author of five books, including Sew a Beautiful Gift.

Buying a Serger

by Rita Opseth

Many busy home sewers are looking for ways to save time but are not willing to sacrifice quality. Sergers offer the special stitches of ready-to-wear with faster and easier construction methods. These machines sew seams at about 1500 stitches per minute, simultaneously trimming and overcasting the raw edges for quality seam finishes. Used side by side with your conventional sewing machine, a serger can add new appeal and excitement to home sewing.

Sergers are excellent for stitching knit seams with built-in stretch, which makes T-shirts, swimwear, and lingerie fast and easy to sew. Sergers also excel at sewing all types of woven fabrics, from sheers and silkies to heavy denims.

The special overlock stitches available on sergers are not limited to the narrow self-finished seams and overcast edge finishes. In addition to these basic stitches, rolled hems, blindstitched hems, and decorative flatlocking features are also available on some models.

Many educators and dealers say that sergers are to sewing what microwaves are to cooking. Even though sergers don't replace your conventional sewing machine any more than microwaves replace conventional ranges, it's also true that once you own a microwave and a serger, you wonder how you ever lived without them.

I prefer comparing sergers with computers. Just as buying and operating a computer requires more research and training than required for a typewriter, you'll need to do a little homework before you buy and operate a serger. But the payoff and rewards are worth it, as you'll see with your finished garments.

How Sergers Work

At first glance, sergers appear complicated. They may use up to five spools of thread, and they use loopers instead of bobbins to form the stitches. Depending on the model, sergers may have one or two needles.

Serger needle plates, presser feet, and feed dogs work together to move fabric quickly and smoothly with even feeding, preventing puckered seams even on the sheerest fabrics. Stitch fingers are the small projections on the needle plates and on some presser feet. Stitches are formed around the stitch fingers;

with correct thread tension, the width of the stitch finger determines the width of the stitch.

Models & Stitches

Depending on the model, sergers may use from two to five threads to form stitches. Each type of serger gets its name from all the stitches it has to offer; for example, a 4/3 serger can sew either a 4-thread or a 3-thread stitch.

In deciding which serger you should buy, determine which one will offer you most of the stitches you want without exceeding your price range. Additional stitches will cost extra. How frequently you plan to use each stitch will help you decide on the right serger. Remember, you will still have your conventional sewing machine to meet some of your needs.

If you are shopping for your first serger, you may find that a serger with several stitch selections will seem too complicated. Do not purchase a serger that you feel is more than you can handle. If your friends own sergers, it will help to talk with them. Demonstrations by two or three dealers will help clear up the differences among the types of sergers. Some dealers may have rental sergers or classes available to help you become more familiar with sergers. Here is a brief description of each type of serger and the stitches they create.

2-thread sergers form only one type of stitch and are more limited in their use than other sergers. The stitches are formed by one needle and one looper. They make neat, lightweight seam finishes and require only two spools of thread. The stitches may also be used for flatlock decorative seaming and give the best results in blind hemming because of the lightweight finish.

3-thread sergers form stitches with one needle and upper and lower loopers. The complete stretch of 3-thread stitches makes it suitable for seaming and for seam finishes on many fabrics, including wovens and one-way or two-way stretch knits. Some 3-thread sergers, called 3/2 models, convert to sew the 2-thread stitch. Most 3-thread sergers also have flatlock capabilities.

4-thread sergers vary depending on the model of serger. The 4/2 model forms the 2-thread stitch described above as an edge finish; two additional threads simultaneously stitch a 2-thread chainstitch at the seamline. The chainstitch does not stretch and will ravel as on flour bags when the thread is broken,

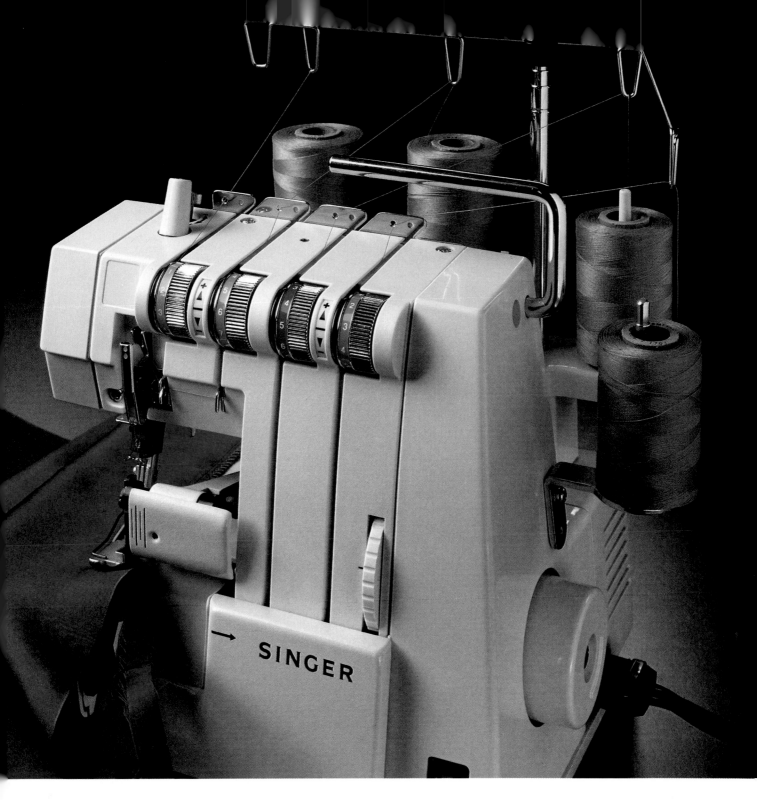

but it is useful for woven fabrics and straight seams, such as those on draperies. The 2-thread chainstitch or the 2-thread overedge may be used separately.

The 4/3 model forms the 3-thread stitch, with a fourth thread adding another row of stitches. The extra thread makes a more stable and durable seam with less stretch than a 3-thread stitch. It is a more durable seam for stable knits and woven garments subject to stress. The 4/3 serger will sew a 3-thread seam when the fourth thread is eliminated; the 4/3/2 model also converts to a 2-thread stitch.

5-thread sergers form a 2-thread chainstitch at the seamline plus a 3-thread overlock stitch, producing wide stitches that are stable for nonstretch seams. On 5/3/2 models, the chainstitch may be eliminated, converting to a 3-thread stitch for stretch seams; the 2-thread chainstitch may also be used separately.

5/4/3/2 models have more stitches than any other serger on the market. In addition to the stitches on the 5/3/2 model, this machine does a 4-thread stitch consisting of a 2-thread chainstitch and a 2-thread overedge. Either stitch may also be used alone.

Flatlock stitching, bottom; rolled hem, top.

Flatlock stitches are decorative stitches used for creativity and special effects on sportswear and other garments. These stitches can also be used on sweater knits for seams that do not twist and on tricot for lingerie seams with less bulk.

Any serger with an adequate range of tension adjustment can be used for flatlock stitching. The machine is threaded with either two or three threads, and the tension is adjusted to create decorative seaming that lies flat. Have this feature demonstrated by your dealer. If the stitches do not lie as flat and even as desired, the tension may need to be readjusted or the tension range of that serger may be inadequate.

Rolled hem stitching is available on many models. To produce these narrow hems, the serger trims away any raveling, rolls under the raw edge, and overcasts with tiny stitches. Some brands offer built-in rolled hem features; on other brands a screwdriver is used to install a different needle plate and presser foot. If the rolled hem accessory is a separate part, it may also be sold separately as an option. Keep in mind that unless this feature is easy to use, you may avoid using it and not get the full value. If this is a feature you want, test the tension on the serger before you buy to ensure that it is adequately adjustable to give a nicely rolled edge.

Features of a Serger

Once you have decided which stitches are important to you and which type of serger you want, you will find that additional features will vary somewhat from one brand to another. Here again, you must evaluate your own needs to get the best value.

Some features, used as selling points, may be overrated by dealers and fall into the category of gimmicks you'll seldom need. You may also find that dealers and manufacturers sing praises of a feature that virtually all brands have in common, such as color coding and presser foot lifter. You may even hear contradictory reports, such as whether conventional or industrial needles are best.

Built-in light is essential for sewing accuracy. The work area around the needle and knife should be well lit. An additional overhead light is also helpful.

Power safety switch shuts off electrical power without requiring that the cord be unplugged. This switch may also control the built-in light.

Rotary or oscillator-style mechanical action may be used. The main consideration is the performance of the specific serger and how smoothly it handles at your usual sewing speed.

Color-coded threading is available on virtually all makes and models to identify the path each thread takes for proper threading. Knowing how to thread the serger is crucial, because sergers will not sew correctly unless threaded properly.

Self-threading lower loopers simplify threading on some sergers. The lower looper is often the most difficult part to thread; pay special attention to how it is threaded.

Slide-in threading or easy-to-thread hooks are features on some sergers. It is true that a serger should be easy to thread, but it is equally important that it stay threaded. Check that threads do not "jump" out of the guides during high-speed sewing because they are not adequately secured in place.

Needles may be conventional or industrial. The make and model of the serger will determine which is used. Conventional needles are the same size needles used in conventional sewing machines. Most industrial needles have round shanks and are more difficult to insert. A new flat-shank industrial needle is now available for some sergers. It is easier to insert than round-shank needles.

On some sergers with two needles, both needles may be secured with one screw. Replacing needles or changing to single-needle operation is easier if each needle is held by its own screw.

Upper and lower knives are features on all sergers. The knives work together as scissors to trim raw edges of fabric. Most upper knives can be moved out of position to prevent cutting when it is not desired or to make needle threading easier. Knives on sergers are replaced, not sharpened, when dull. Inserting knives is similar to changing sewing machine needles. The cutting edge of the knives should be clearly visible for accurate serging, just as you must see the blade of scissors to cut accurately. The knives on any serger may be used to cut thread ends; some brands also offer thread cutters.

Finger guards and other safety features are available on virtually all sergers. I have not heard of an instance when anyone has been cut or injured with serger knives, which is the primary concern for most people.

Handwheels may turn forward or backward, depending on the brand. It is important on any serger that you turn the handwheel in the direction it is meant to be turned. If it rotates in a direction different from that of your conventional machine, it may take a little getting used to, but most people adjust quite easily.

Stitch width of a serged stitch is the distance in millimeters from the raw edge of the fabric to the needle thread on 2-thread and 3-thread stitches; on 4-thread and 5-thread stitches, it is the distance from the raw edge to the left needle thread.

Stitch width adjustments can be made on some models as easily as turning a dial. On most 4/3 sergers with two needles, the width of the 3-thread stitch is changed to a narrower stitch by removal of the left needle. This adjustment gives two choices for the width of stitch, whereas dial adjustments are completely variable. Still other sergers give no stitch width choice, or as little change as 0.5 mm.

Stitch width range may vary from as narrow as 2.5 mm to as wide as 8.5 mm, depending on the model. Use this general rule for determining the right stitch width: for fine fabrics, use fine, narrow stitches; for heavy fabrics, use wider heavy stitches. Having a broader range of stitch widths will allow you to sew on a greater variety of fabrics without requiring additional conventional stitching to support the stitches.

Stitch length is the distance between stitches. All sergers have a reasonable stitch length range, but some sergers have the advantage of very close satin stitches.

Snap-on presser feet save time and effort when it is necessary to change presser feet; however, presser feet are not changed as frequently on a serger as on conventional machines.

Blind hem foot helps feed the hemline accurately for stitches that are nearly invisible, using a 2-thread or 3-thread flatlock stitch. The foot may be an optional attachment and is not available for all sergers.

Taping foot or guide acts as a third hand in guiding narrow tapes or ribbons as the serger stitches along the tape. The feature is used for stabilizing seams or applying decorative ribbons. This feature is helpful but has a limited use.

Elastic foot guides and stretches narrow elastic as it is stitched. The ratio of elastic to fabric is adjusted manually, and the setting will vary depending on the elastic. When deciding whether to buy this attachment, be aware that elastic can be applied easily without it. Also consider how often you will serge elastic and how easily the attachment is adjusted.

Waste containers are a helpful accessory. Trimming seams with a serger creates clippings, which are dispensed into the container.

Differential feed prevents puckered seams on lightweight fabrics, such as sheers and tricots, and eliminates stretched-out seams on sweater knits, crosswise knit grains, and bias edges. The feature functions well but adds considerably to the cost of the serger. Realize that some sergers handle these fabrics well without this feature, so before making a purchase use various weights and types of fabrics to test each model you are considering. When problems with puckering occur on a serger, loosening the needle thread tension or holding the fabric taut is usually all that is needed to eliminate the puckering. For fabrics that tend to stretch out of shape, lightening the pressure on the presser foot is often the solution. If you are willing to use these sewing techniques or if you seldom sew these fabrics, you may find that you can save money by doing without this feature. But if you sew many sweater knits or sheers, it may be worthwhile to invest more in a serger with differential feed.

The Dealer

The dealers you go to will be a key element in your decision, and the dealer you buy from will play a big part in the satisfaction you have with your serger. Most factory-authorized dealers have more than one model to offer of that brand and have inventory in stock.

Some dealers may offer special prices on sergers, whereas other dealers may charge a bit more and include training or classes on how to operate the machine. Serging methods are different from conventional methods, and as a new owner you will need someone to guide you through the learning process. A dealer who is concerned about your learning process is essential to a satisfying experience with your first serger purchase.

Testing the Serger

- Assemble fabrics of several weights and types you want to sew. Have the dealers demonstrate, using these fabrics. Check to see whether the machine stitches with perfect tension on a wide variety of fabrics without requiring tension adjustments.

- Save and label stitch samples with the model name and number to compare stitch quality.

- Have the dealer explain stitches available on the serger and adjustments required for changing from one stitch to another.

- Have the dealer explain tension adjustments and stitch width and length adjustments.

- Have all features and accessories explained and demonstrated.

- Have the dealer completely thread the machine.

- Ask questions along the way to be sure each step is clear in your mind.

- Test the foot control to see if it works smoothly. You should feel in control of the speed.

- Be sure the workspace is well lit, so you can see exactly where the needle enters the fabric.

- Draw a few lines on a piece of fabric (or use a striped fabric). Practice cutting exactly on a line; then stitch so the needle runs along a line.

- Turn each of the tension dials a little at a time. Check stitching to see how it is affected. If a drastic change in tension occurs with a slight movement of

the dial, you will not be able to fine-tune the tension. Dialing the perfect stitch is similar to tuning in a radio station for good reception.

- Try turning the tension dials at random; then see how easily you can restore the perfect stitch with your dealer's assistance.

- Thread the machine yourself from start to finish. The dealer may show you how to thread the machine "by tying threads on," but it is still important that you are capable of threading the machine completely.

- Run the serger at all speed levels, including high speed. Check for stitch quality, and check threading after high-speed sewing to see whether any threads have "jumped" out of a thread guide.

- Test accessories.

The Purchase

Once you have made your decision about which serger to buy, remember that the only machine that matters is the one "with your name on it." Be sure it works every bit as well as the one you saw demonstrated.

Serger stitches, left to right: 5-thread, 4/3-thread, 4/2-thread, 3-thread, 2-thread.

Allow extra time the day you purchase your serger. Before you carry it home, unpack the box at the store to examine your serger. Here are a few tips on what to look for:

• Be sure the machine is threaded correctly; threads often become tangled in packing. Your dealer can help you to straighten threads, if necessary.

• Stitch on a few fabrics to check the tension. Sergers are factory set; but if the tension is not perfect, have it readjusted by your dealer.

• Oil the serger at the time of the purchase. Sergers that have been stored for more than a few months will require oil.

• Sign up for training classes right away.

After the Purchase

It is your responsibility to care for your serger, cleaning and oiling as described in your manual. Change needles and knives as necessary to ensure good stitching and cutting performance. When your serger is cared for properly, you may expect years of fine performance.

Serger Tips

Use high-quality thread for high-quality stitches. Good thread is especially important to a new owner to avoid stitching problems.

Use your serger immediately to be sure it is performing correctly while it is under warranty.

Sew a variety of garments so you try all stitches and features, including rolled hems and flatlocking.

Become familiar with tension adjustments.

Report any problems to your dealer. Many problems will be "operator malfunction" or "pilot error." In these cases, your dealer can help you solve problems with a little training and advice.

Allow yourself to be a beginner. Expand your sewing experiences by using new fabrics and fashions unsuitable for conventional methods. After years of sewing on conventional sewing machines, you'll find it exciting to learn new methods.

Rita Opseth is on staff with the Singer Sewing Reference Library. Her experience includes director of educational programs for a retail fabric chain and instructor, speaker, and writer specializing in serging.

Add a Knitting Machine to Your Sewing Room

by Peggy Bendel

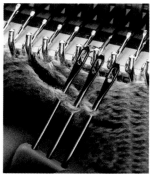

If you sew, this is an excellent time to look at what knitting machines have to offer. Mixing knitted and woven fabrics within a garment is a leading designer detail. An ongoing fashion theme is the complete knitwear wardrobe that spans the seasons and works for multiple occasions. A knitting machine not only equips you to follow trends such as these, but also enables you to combine knitting and sewing for creative clothing treatments.

With a knitting machine you can make collars, cuffs, and ribbing bands to customize sewn tops and dresses. You can knit richly textured sleeves for a synthetic suede jacket or a handsome lining for a reversible quilted vest. With one of the most sophisticated machine models, you can trace motifs directly from a printed fabric for a one-of-a-kind skirt and sweater set. Even a basic knitting machine can turn out yards of original fabrics to cut and sew from the patterns of your choice.

What a Knitting Machine Does

Different models vary in features, but all knitting machines work essentially the same way. There are two basic parts: the needle bed and the carriage.

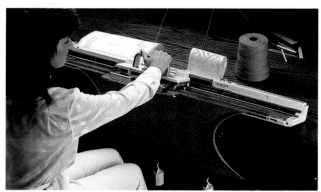

The needle bed consists of ninety or more needles, depending on the model. The needles are not like hand knitting needles, but are similar to latch hooks. They slide back and forth in slots on the needle bed.

The carriage moves on a track from one side to the other across the needle bed and delivers yarn to the needles. The carriage also slides the needles back

and forth so hinged latches on the needles can link loops of yarn to make knitted fabric. You move the carriage by hand in an ironing-style motion; an entire row of stitches is knitted in seconds with each pass of the carriage.

Compared with hand knitting, where you knit one stitch at a time on two needles, machine knitting is fast. But from a creative point of view, the greatest advantage of machine knitting is how easily you can substitute yarns and combine different yarns for original effects. Most knitwear is simply shaped. You can change the total look of a standard garment just by using a novel yarn or setting the machine to produce an attractive stitch texture.

Shopping for Your First Machine

Knitting machines are not new; in fact, they've been available since the 1930s. Yarn shops are a natural place to ask about knitting machines, but recent developments in home sewing indicate knitters' haunts are not the only sources to consider.

More and more retailers who cater to sewers are now carrying knitting machines and supplies. Because fashion emphasizes knits, all the major home sewing pattern companies have established knitting programs and publish project instructions in the form of leaflets, magazines, or paper patterns. Getting started in machine knitting doesn't have to take you into an unfamiliar setting or introduce you to unknown brand names; you might find everything you need in shops you normally patronize.

Still, shopping for your first knitting machine can be confusing. One line of machines does not parallel another, making valid comparisons difficult. Manufacturers have different names to identify important features and accessories. Some manufacturers build capabilities into their machines that other manufacturers offer as attachments you must purchase.

You can pay under $200 or more than $1500 for a knitting machine. Consider what you will use the machine for and what features you will need. It's easy to become dazzled by new electronic features you may never use. On the other hand, you don't want to purchase a machine that quickly becomes inadequate for your purposes. There are many options and accessories to upgrade basic models so you can make improvements if necessary, but the add-ons are costly. It's possible to spend as much on accessories as for the original machine.

Standard & Bulky Gauge Machines

When shopping for a knitting machine, you must first decide whether you want a standard or bulky gauge machine.

A *standard gauge* machine can handle fine, lightweight yarns such as fingering, baby, and sport weights. This machine produces a light to mediumweight, supple knitted fabric suitable for sweaters, dresses, skirts, and many other garments. It's a type of knit flattering to many figures because it is not thick. A standard gauge machine also makes better ribbings for finishing edges and is generally more suitable for making intricate stitch patterns and detailed multi-colored designs. There's a long list of options and accessories available for standard gauge machines.

A *bulky gauge* machine can handle worsted and heavier weight yarns, as well as most of the fashion novelty yarns used by hand knitters. It produces a thicker, heavier knitted fabric that is most appropriate for sweaters, coats, and similar garments. Bulky knits more closely resemble hand knits than do standard gauge knits. Thicker yarn makes the knitting go faster, and since bulky machines are relatively simple in features and options, they are easier to master and less expensive than standard gauge machines.

It's a good idea to browse through several fashion knitting magazines before you shop for a knitting machine. Clip or mark the knit fashions you would like to make. This will help you decide which gauge machine to select. As you become more involved in machine knitting, you may want to own both.

If you compare different needle beds, you can fine-tune your choice. For example, the number of needles per bed varies; the more needles in the bed, the wider the fabric you can knit. This feature is more important on bulky than on standard gauge machines because an additional twenty needles may mean less than 1" (2.5 cm) of fabric when using a fine fingering yarn but can mean 2" (5 cm) or more when using a thick, bulky yarn.

Beds also differ in needle pitch, the space between the needles. Most standard gauge machines have a pitch of 4.5 mm; and most bulkies, 9 mm. A wider pitch allows you to use a wider choice of yarns. A narrower pitch means that a more specific group of yarns can be used.

Single & Double Needle Beds

If you have decided to buy a standard gauge machine, the second decision you will have to make is whether to purchase a single bed or a double bed model. A *single bed* machine may be all you need, at least to start. You can make numerous stitch patterns on a single bed machine and manually perform techniques such as making ribbing. You work ribbing stitches a stitch at a time, using a latch tool furnished with the machine.

Double needle bed machines cost more, but they can save you time. On a double bed machine, you work ribbing a row at a time using the carriage. A second needle bed also greatly expands the number of stitch patterns and knitted textures you can create.

Ask the dealer to demonstrate making ribbing on both types of machines so you can see the difference. Making ribbing is something you will do repeatedly in machine knitting, just as you commonly make buttonholes when sewing by machine.

The single or double bed decision isn't binding, because most single bed machines can be converted by purchasing a *ribber bed*, an attachment that is simply a second needle bed. Industry studies show that the great majority of single bed machine owners purchase a ribber within the first year. The price of a single bed machine plus a ribber is slightly less than the cost of a double bed machine, and a correctly mounted ribber bed attachment can be as precise as a double bed machine.

Extras for Easier Creative Knitting

A number of extras are available that make it easier to knit various stitch patterns and decorative motifs. Depending on brand and model, these may be options to purchase separately, built-in features, or accessories that are included.

Two important extras involve needle selection. On a basic model, you must stop after each row to pull forth or push back the needles in the sequence required to form the stitch pattern. Usually this maneuver is done with a hand-held metal or plastic tool that resembles a giant comb.

With a *punchcard patterning* device, you simply insert a card that has a sequence of holes the carriage "reads" to select the needles. As you pass the carriage across the needle bed, the card moves up a notch for each row knitted and is ready to automatically select the needles for the next row in the pattern.

A *programmable patterning* system also selects needles for stitch patterns automatically, but you enter the stitch pattern by means of a calculator-style key pad or by inserting a printed pattern card into an electronic sensor. Both punchcard and programmable stitch patterns are geometric; the stitch pattern is mapped on a grid or chart. The size of the maximum pattern repeat varies from one brand to another; the fewer stitches in the maximum pattern repeat, the smaller the stitch pattern must be.

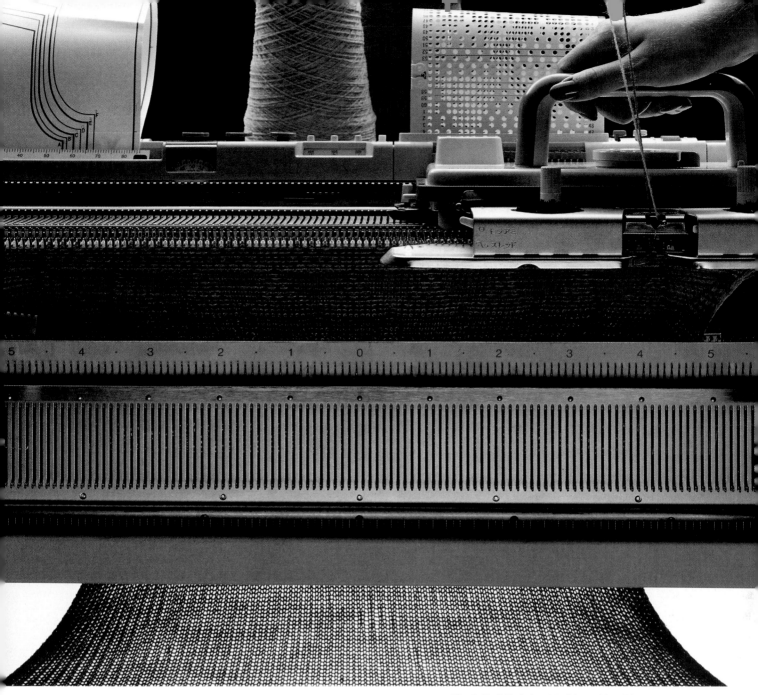

Single Bed Knitting Machine with Ribber Attachment

On top-of-the-line models, programmable patterning systems are quite versatile. You can spread the stitch pattern across the entire garment section and create nonrepetitious designs. On certain models, you can use a special stylus to draw freehand or trace motifs for multi-colored stitch patterns that the machine will knit automatically. You know a machine has state-of-the-art programmability when the maximum stitch repeat is the full width of the needle bed.

Other extras worth considering simplify certain techniques. For example, to transfer the stitches from one needle bed to another to work ribbing or other stitch patterns on a double bed machine, you can use the special tool furnished with the machine and do it by hand, or you can use a *transfer carriage* and do it automatically in much less time.

To make stitch patterns with eyelets or spaces as part of the design, you can move the stitches to adjacent needles manually, or use a *lace carriage* and transfer the stitches automatically.

To knit intarsia designs, a popular type of knitting that involves motifs knitted into the fabric in blocks of color, you may appreciate an *intarsia carriage*. After knitting each row of stitches, this carriage brings the needles forward automatically for the next row, so you do not have to do this manually.

To make multi-colored stitch patterns, many knitting machines have a built-in *two-color yarn changer*. For machines without this feature, adding an accessory *four-color yarn changer* allows you to thread up to four yarns through tension guides, so colors can conveniently be brought into the knitting.

Extras to Simplify Garment Shaping

Unless you are knitting straight fabric yardage on the machine, you will have to increase and decrease stitches to shape garment sections, most notably at the sleeve cap, armhole, and neckline. On a basic knitting machine, you must keep track of the rows and stitches by following written instructions or a scale model drawing of the garment section.

A *mechanical shaping* device allows you to use printed patterns. You roll the pattern into the shaping device as if inserting paper into a typewriter; every time the machine knits a row, the pattern moves up one line. The number of stitches to increase or decrease can be very easily read from the ruler at the bottom edge of the shaping device. The patterns eliminate guesswork and can be altered for a perfect fit in the same way you alter tissue sewing patterns.

A *programmable shaping* system does a similar job electronically. Most programs store basic garment section shapes, although you can use the system to make original shapes, too. You enter your figure measurements and select the garment shape by means of a calculator-style key pad. No paper patterns are used. The system sizes the garment automatically to your figure measurements, keeps track of the stitches and rows, and displays the knit shaping instructions.

Evaluate the Dealership

In many respects, the knitting machine dealer is almost as important as the knitting machine. Explore the dealer's arrangements for repairs and servicing. Examine model garments on display to judge the capabilities of the machine. Check if yarns, patterns, and other supplies are available so you can gather project materials conveniently. Ask whether the dealer offers introductory lessons and has an ongoing education program, so you can learn more advanced techniques as your interest grows. Dealers may sponsor knitting clubs, which meet for idea exchange between fellow knitters.

After all, knitting by machine, like sewing by machine, can become a lifelong pursuit; it seems there's always something new to learn and try. Although a machine makes knitting faster and easier, a few lessons and your first pullover sweater will not make you an expert. With friendly support from the dealer and your own willingness to practice and experiment, you could discover an absorbing new craft that's the perfect complement to your sewing expertise.

Peggy Bendel has written seven books and more than 300 magazine articles on sewing-related topics. She is a contributing editor of Sew News.

Shaping with Shoulder Pads
by Clotilde

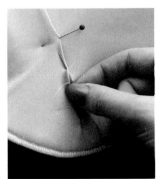

A bewildering collection of shoulder pads is available in fabric stores. Choose from washable or dryclean-only; from uncovered pads or those covered with nylon tricot or acetate; or from permanently molded contour polyester pads, foam pads, or polyester fiberfill pads. There are styles for blouses, jackets, or raglan sleeves in thicknesses varying from ¼" to 1½" (6 mm to 3.8 cm). Commercial shoulder pads can be purchased from tailors' supply houses. These are generally dryclean-only as they are made of cotton batting that becomes lumpy when washed. Patterns to make your own shoulder pads are available in pattern books.

It is important to check the pattern envelope for the suggested shoulder pad thickness. Patternmakers allow extra room at the shoulder for 1" (2.5 cm) shoulder pads. If you decide to use a ½" (1.3 cm)

pad, there may be a vacant space unless you have very square shoulders that compensate for thinner pads. Change the pattern to allow for thinner pads by stitching shoulder seams ½" (1.3 cm) deeper at the armhole edge. Be sure to reduce sleeve cap ease proportionately, as the armhole is now 1" (2.5 cm) smaller. If this seems like too much work, use 1" (2.5 cm) pads.

Uncovered pads are used in lined jackets and coats. Use covered shoulder pads in dresses, blouses, sweaters, and unlined jackets. Purchased covered pads are covered with nylon tricot or acetate. Some come with hook and loop strips that make them removable. This extra work makes them more expensive than uncovered pads. Save money by covering pads with lining fabric or flesh-colored nylon tricot. A nylon stocking makes a perfect cover to reduce shadowing through with light fabrics.

Clotilde is a nationally recognized sewing authority, author, lecturer, and TV host. She founded her mail-order notions company, Clotilde, Inc., in 1972.

How to Cover Shoulder Pads

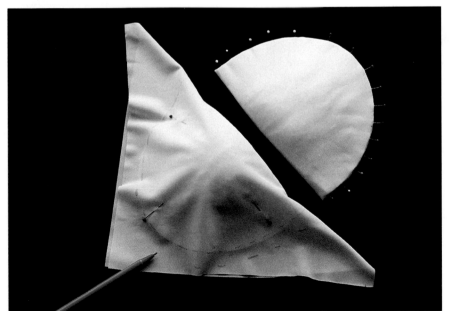

1) Cut a 12" (30.5 cm) square of fabric. Place pad on fabric with armhole edge along the diagonal. Fold fabric over pad. You now have all-bias fabric that easily shapes to pad. Draw outline of pad, add ⅝" (1.5 cm) seam allowance, and cut. Serge around edges. Or fold seam allowances in on underside of pad, and slipstitch around cut edges.

2) Slipstitch a dart in underside to hold in contoured shape. Tack pointed ends to armhole seam allowances and rounded portion to shoulder seam.

Pressing Update

by Claire Shaeffer

Proper pressing is essential for professional sewing results, and with the latest state-of-the-art equipment, pressing is easier than ever. This overview of pressing aids introduces some of the newest items available to home sewers.

Professional irons (**a**) are at the top of the list. Designed for tailors and small manufacturers, Hi-Steam and Sussman gravity feed irons are now available to home sewers. The most important feature is the ability to produce high-pressure blasts of hot, dry steam.

The iron has a separate reservoir, which must be hung from a ceiling or wall bracket above the iron. This reservoir will hold enough unheated tap water to steam continuously for eight hours or more.

Other features include a conveniently located large steam control, which is easy to use for long periods without tiring. The iron steams in any position: vertically, horizontally, and upside down; and it has a wider temperature range than household models.

Some disadvantages are the lack of portability, a temperature control that does not indicate settings for fabric types, and cost. Some models are wired for right-handed pressers only. It is reasonable to expect many years of service after the warranty expires.

Regular household irons have changed tremendously in recent years, and although many of the new features have been welcomed by the average user, they aren't especially attractive to home sewers. In fact, the most popular feature, the automatic shutoff, will drive you crazy. The iron turns off if you don't use it again within 10 to 15 minutes, depending on the model.

Here are some more of my complaints about household irons: the temperature range is too narrow; the water capacity, too small. The steam blasts are weak and too wet, water always spills when I'm shaping over a ham, and the iron isn't heavy enough for fusing. Cordless irons don't hold their heat. Worst of all, the iron usually dies the day after the warranty expires.

The Rowenta **(b)**, imported from Germany, is a new entry to the home iron market. It is quick-heating, and it has an extra-wide heel rest and large soleplate. Controls are centrally located, a must for left-handers. It features a "burst of steam," an essential for the home sewer, and best of all, a three-year warranty.

The Vin-Max Puff iron **(c)** has a unique oval heating surface fixed on the top of a clamp. It is especially useful for pressing hard-to-reach sections, ruffles, gathered skirts, puffed sleeves, children's garments, and smocked designs. This gadget can be set up near your sewing machine for press-as-you-go sewing.

A Steamstress steamer **(d)** has a plastic soleplate that doesn't heat. It is particularly useful for pressing fabrics that shine, scorch, or melt easily. Since it is lightweight and works well when held vertically or horizontally, it is useful for pressing draperies and finished garments.

The ironing press **(e)** has a large heating sole, several times the size of an ordinary iron, its own padded board, and an optional hundred pounds of pressure. The press is well suited for fusing interfacings, pressing embroidered and appliquéd articles, setting pleats and creases, pressing yardage, and blocking knits, as well as the usual household ironing.

The Teflon soleplate **(f)** is an easily attached sole, which can be used instead of a press cloth to avoid iron shine, sticking, and scorching when pressing from the right side of the fabric.

The Velvaboard™ **(g)** is a pressing pad with a moderately stiff pile. Use it for pressing velvet, velveteen, corduroy, and embroidered fabrics.

Cotton ironing board covers and grain cloths are 100 percent cotton and printed with grainlines. These pressing covers are especially helpful for pressing during construction, and the all-cotton fabric absorbs the moisture so the fashion fabric will dry quickly. Unfortunately, they are much more expensive than regular ironing board covers. To enjoy the advantages at a fraction of the price, I covered my ironing board with all-cotton gingham woven with 1" (2.5 cm) squares.

The traditional ironing board cover has a reflective surface designed to make ironing faster. In addition to limiting the control that you have when pressing, the cover slows the drying process when you're shaping with steam. More important, it can reflect the steam enough to cause burns and damage some fabrics.

Sources:
The Fabric Carr, 170 State St., Los Altos, CA 94022; catalog, SASE. *June Tailor, Inc.,* Box 208, Richfield, WI 53076; catalog, 50 cents. *Nancy's Notions®,* Box 683, Beaver Dam, WI 53916; catalog, free. *Trovato Sewing Catalog,* 1741 First Ave. So., Seattle, WA 98134; catalog, $1 refundable with first order.

Claire Shaeffer has taught garment construction and fashion design classes in college and adult programs. She is the author of five books, including The Complete Book of Sewing Smart.

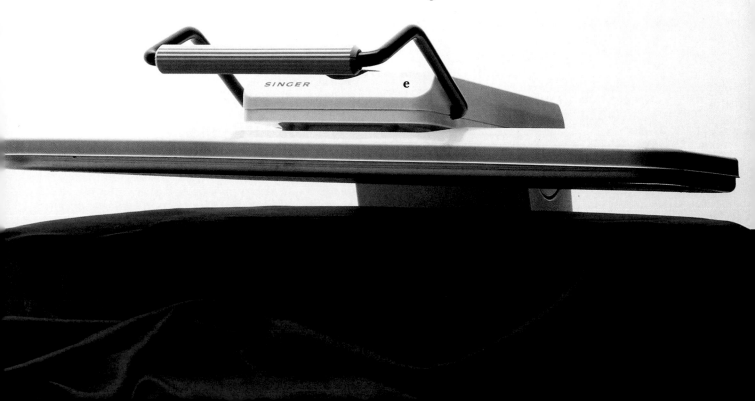

The Best New Sewing Notions —
More Than Just Gadgets

by David Page Coffin

I admit it. I'm a sucker for a sewing gadget. I've got dozens of them. Someone is always coming up with a clever solution to some sewing problem, and I don't want to miss a single one. Many of them I confess I don't use. But some of these gadgets are so good that I couldn't sew without them; they deserve to be called *tools*. In fact, I think three major areas of home sewing have been completely revolutionized by tools that weren't in the average sewing basket ten years ago.

The three areas are cutting, marking, and basting, and the tools are rotary cutters, water-soluble markers, and glue sticks. If you haven't tried these, you're not sewing as efficiently as you could be. There are lots of wonderful new gadgets besides these, but more on them later.

Rotary Cutters & Mats

The rotary cutter **(a)** has my vote for the best thing to hit home sewers since the sewing machine — but most sewers don't even use one. The rotary cutter is not just for quilters, even though that's how they are marketed. I cut out every garment I make entirely with

a rotary cutter, and I use one for almost all seam trimming and grading. Scissors just don't compare. Rotary cutters are twice as fast and twice as accurate.

There is no way you can cut out two identical layers of fabric with scissors. The blade underneath will always distort the layers. We've lived with this before, but rotary cutters eliminate it. You can cut a perfect straight line with a rotary and a ruler as fast as you can draw it, and you can cut a curved line as quickly and as smoothly as you can run over it with a tracing wheel. Nothing is better for cleaning up frayed fabric edges. Try a rotary cutter and say good-bye to ragged cuts, pattern pieces that almost match, and cutting out that takes all day.

Cutters all work equally well. They come in two sizes; the larger one is better for thick fabrics, the smaller one for tight curves. One cutter is made so that the blade (razor sharp!) is exposed only when you're pressing down on the fabric, a good idea that doesn't interfere with the cutting action at all. Others have blade covers that snap up or down, but they also have adjustable guide arms **(b)** that allow you to cut a precise distance away from a pattern piece or ruler. I find that this feature is essential, perfect for adding seam allowances and for simple adjustments.

When you cut with a rotary, use a firm, smooth stroke. You shouldn't have to saw back and forth along the

Mats come in many sizes (even round) up to 48" by 96" (122 by 244 cm) and in three thicknesses. Thin will probably be suitable for most sewers' needs. Select medium or heavy thicknesses for extended life. Keep mats from direct sunlight and high temperatures.

A number of quilter's rulers are designed for use with a rotary cutter, but at 24" (61 cm) they just aren't long enough for garments. My solution was simple. Most towns have Plexiglas dealers who will cut to order any shape you want. I bought a 3" by 36" (7.5 by 91.5 cm) piece with finished edges for under $5, and put a transparent stick-on measuring tape on it. It works like a charm. Don't overlook art stores for small rulers, curves, and triangles. The smaller quilter's rulers are great for seam trimming, and some are designed to simplify cutting mitered corners. A lip edge (e) on one ruler allows it to work as a T-square. Any rulers you get should be transparent (f), at least 3" (7.5 cm) wide for safe and firm holding when you cut, and at least 1/8" (3 mm) thick, or have a metal edge (g) so the cutter won't nick the edge.

Weighing down pattern pieces with weights (h) instead of pinning them down works well with rotary cutting. It's much faster and there's no distortion. Sometimes weights can interfere with rulers, so I just use my collection of rulers, curves, and triangles as weights, particularly around the edges of patterns.

I hope you will try a rotary cutter for garment cutting. It's a real breakthrough!

Markers

Sewers need a mark that is easy to put on, easy to see, easy to get off, but stays put until they're done with it. I use water-soluble markers (i) whenever I'm going to wash the garment I'm making. They have all the advantages I've listed, plus they make a small, accurate mark. On all-cottons I've never had the marks last through a wash, or come back afterward, even if a drop of water didn't do the trick right away. For dark fabrics washout pencil markers in white or red both work well when used lightly, but usually must be washed to vanish completely. I don't like disappearing markers, because the marks often fade before I'm through with them, especially if the pen has been around for a while.

Quilters have many tales of washout and disappearing marks reappearing, or even eating holes in the fabric a year or so down the road if not thoroughly washed out, so I'm very cautious on dryclean-only fabrics. Testing is a good idea, but who can wait a year for the results? If your fabric is not washable, the best marker is probably chalk.

Chalk wheels (j) are the latest thing, and they work beautifully. Test to make sure the marks really brush out completely, and if they will last long enough to be

cutting line. Don't feel that you must cut as fast as possible. Take it slow and steady, be sure before you cut, and you'll save time. Use a ruler or a curve whenever possible.

The rotary cutter's problem is that by itself it's only half the tool. To use it properly and economically, you need a cutting surface that won't dull the blades, that protects your table, and that's big enough for garment pieces — at least 48" (122 cm) long, or more.

Most cutting mats describe themselves as "self-healing." The mats don't actually heal; what that term means is that cuts are invisible — no ridges or tracks are left behind, but the cut is still there. The softer the mats the easier they are on your blades, but also the harder it is to cut on them. I was unable to cut through two layers of silk crepe de chine on a soft mat. The blade just pushed the cloth into the mat.

Mats may be gridded (c) or plain (d). The grids are helpful for cutting straight lines and fabric strips. Mats can be used on either side. Some have a pebbled surface on one side, which prevents slippery fabrics from shifting.

Mats are available in green, white, black, or translucent. Green reduces light glare, especially when large sizes are used. Black is used for laces and white garments, and is popular in bridal shops. Translucent is good for tracing and graphic projects.

useful. Look for a wheel that puts down a fine line and is easy to refill. Another modern wonder product is a chalk that works like traditional tailor's chalk, but washes out, disappears under an iron, or evaporates within five days.

For many fabrics you've got a free marking tool right at your finger tips — your nails. If your fabric will take a light crease and later release it, you can make a line or cross (to mark a point) by rubbing your nail firmly over the spot. A smooth tracing wheel works well, too, and a hard surface underneath can help you make a clearer mark. I use my nail to mark pivot points when I'm topstitching details with corners.

With all these options, I've found it is almost never necessary to thread-mark, but for fine tailoring and delicate fabrics it's still occasionally the best way. It's all part of the ritual.

Basting

Basting is a ritual that I will go through only at gunpoint. It is necessary, and has no equal, when you must hold complex shapes and multiple layers and keep them flexible at the same time. For simply holding together two pieces of fabric I couldn't do without glue stick. It's as flexible as basting, there are no pins to pull out or to distort the fabric, and it washes out completely. Whenever instructions say, "Pin, baste, and stitch," and the fabric is washable, I reach for the glue stick.

It can, however, turn into a sticky mess if you're not careful. You want only a thin layer, so turn out just a tiny bit and use the tube edge to spread a small dot where you want it. This will work even if the glue has gotten stringy and gummy. I put down a dot every inch (centimeter) or so, press the fabric in place, and iron it dry so it won't shift. If you need to reposition it, just spray it with water; it will soften up and you can try again. Glue stick is perfect for any precise positioning, such as matching plaids or stripes, and situations when you don't want to remove pins as you sew. In humid climates keep the stick in a plastic bag. I've had good results with every brand I've tried, even those sold in stationery stores; just be sure it's washable.

Wash-away basting tapes are available for similar purposes, but I find them more trouble than they are worth. They are tricky to unroll, and they stick to your fingers when you're trying to carefully position them. They are very popular for Ultrasuede®.

Wash-away basting thread (a) is the latest thing, and it is a minor miracle. It's as fine as regular sewing thread, and almost as strong, but will dissolve at a touch of water or steam. You can usually use it just as the top thread, without winding a bobbin, because once the top thread dissolves, there's nothing holding the bobbin thread in place. It is perfect for trial fittings, muslins, and any temporary stitching. I've used it for gathering so I can gather right on the stitching line; I keep the top tension loose and pull the regular bobbin thread. Once dissolved, the regular thread is much easier to pull out, even if it is occasionally caught in the final stitching. If you are very gentle, you can get away with wash-away basting thread on the top and bottom when gathering. Naturally, you can't handle the thread when your hands are moist. Store the thread in two airtight plastic bags if humidity is a problem.

Miscellaneous Essentials

For truly stubborn needles, or anything you need a really good grip on, such as a broken zipper pull, try a needle gripper (b), originally a medical tool called a hemostat, which works like fine needle-nose pliers, except that it locks shut like a mini-vise, so you don't need to keep squeezing. Platinum needles are actually more slippery than ordinary needles, but they are very expensive and just as easily lost as any other needle. The quilter may want to investigate the platinum needle possibilities.

Buttonhole knives (c) are a must. There is no better way to open a buttonhole. Keep the blade covered when not in use, and always use the wooden block — not your rotary mat! I've used mine for over ten years, and it still works fine. If the blade is too long for your buttonhole, just hang the hole halfway off the edge of the block and cut it out in two steps.

A lot of new thimbles are around these days. Two particularly useful ones for sewers are the Bionic Finger (d) and the Thumble™. The Bionic Finger is made of the same stuff as self-healing cutting mats. Besides being a regular thimble, it has a little protrusion in front that has a slit in it. When you wear the Finger on your middle finger, you can easily reach over with your thumb and forefinger and squeeze the slit shut, over the tip of the needle, gripping it securely. Pulling even stuck needles out is easy. Above the protrusion, safely tucked away, is a tiny blade for cutting your thread. Pure genius.

The Thumble is hard plastic. It fits over your thumb and has a little groove to catch the end of the needle, so you can use the thumb's greater strength to push through tough materials. With a little practice, you could probably use the Finger and the Thumble together.

If you love your current thimble, there are still answers for needles that won't pull through easily. Try putting a drop or two of a silicon needle lubricant on a scrap of cloth; touch your needle to it whenever it gets uncooperative.

Bias tape makers (e) automatically and accurately fold to the middle both sides of any fabric strips,

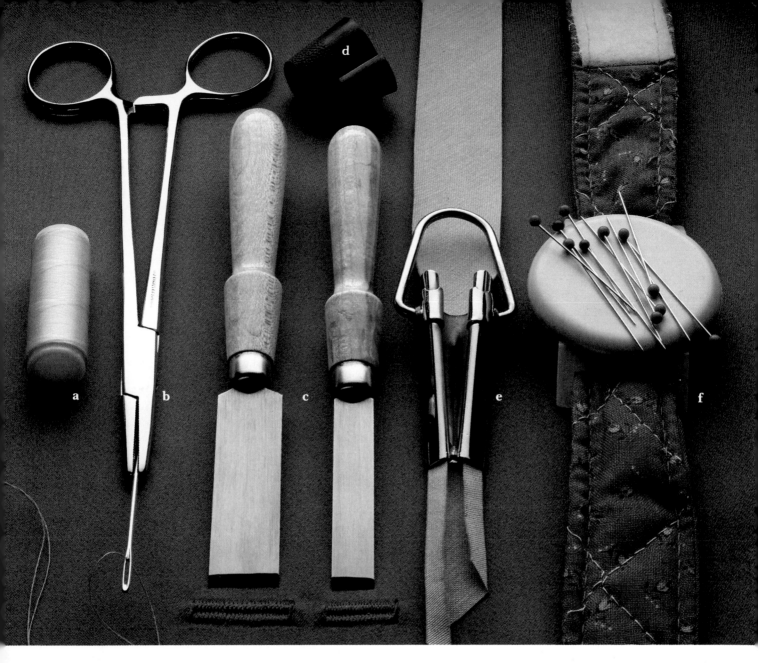

from your rotary cutter, of course. Fold the tape in half again, add a little fusible web, and you've got quick and easy belt loops.

Magnetic pin cushions (**f**) are a sensible idea. Just lightly toss pins at the cushion and they stick. Pick up missed or spilled pins in a flash by holding the cushion over them. When I use pins, I position my cushion behind the machine on the side of the seam that has the pinheads sticking out at a right angle to the seamline. As I pluck out a pin, I toss it at the cushion without missing a stitch. Some computer machines go wild when magnets get too close. Check with your dealer if you've got one of these marvels.

Liquid fray preventer stops fabric edges from raveling, even through the wash. It's great for firming up buttonholes, stopping runs in stockings, and securing knotted threads. Be cautious anywhere the fabric edge will contact skin; the edges get quite stiff. Always test it on a scrap to make sure it's invisible when dry.

Canned compressed air will blow dust and lint out of the tiniest crevice, but it isn't cheap and won't completely remove oily lint, such as the lint in sewing machines. Kids love to play with compressed air, but they can get badly hurt by breathing it or blowing it on their skin, because the air gets cold enough to cause frostbite.

Sources:

Bionic Finger, Box 52, Mt. Hope, OH 44660. *Clotilde, Inc.*, 237 S.W. 28 Street, Ft. Lauderdale, FL 33315; catalog, $1. *Nancy's Notions®*, Box 683, Beaver Dam, WI 53916; catalog, free. *Sewing Emporium*, 1087 Third Ave., Chula Vista, CA 92010; catalog, free. *Thumble, Inc.*, 65-B Division Ave., #333, Eugene, OR 97404. *Treadleart*, 25834 Narbonne Ave., Lomita, CA 90717; catalog, $1.

David Page Coffin is an assistant editor for Threads *magazine. He is also the author of* Custom Shirt Book *and* Custom Making Ties at Home.

Interfacings Update

by Margaret Deck Komives

Interfacings serve several functions. They add support to those areas that need it, promote durability at areas of stress, and add stability to areas that might stretch more than desired. They add shape to some collars and lapels, and crispness to others.

One trend is toward softer, more flexible interfacings. Major designers are showing silk crepe blazers with soft lapels that roll gently. The rigid look is not often found in couture garments. Sof-Shape®, Soft-Fuse™, and Shape-Up, along with weft insertions such as Armo® Weft and Suit-Shape®, are among the more flexible interfacings.

Another trend is the use of mixed weights or a variety of interfacings in one garment, based on the fashion effect desired. With all the varieties available, choosing the right interfacing might seem to be an overwhelming task, but several considerations make the decision easier and the results more satisfactory. The choice should be related to the fashion fabric, the design of the garment, the type of construction, the flexibility desired, and the personal preference of the wearer.

Fashion Fabric & Garment Design

Fabrics vary from sheer to opaque and from soft to crisp. When interfaced, the fabric should retain its original characteristics: drape, color, texture, and stretch. Folding the interfaced fabric back on itself will indicate whether these characteristics are retained; a rounded edge is more desirable than a paperlike crease. A fabric such as crepe de chine should retain its drape, and the interfacing used should allow draping at the same time that it supports the fabric for stability where needed.

Prints of fashion fabrics should not shadow-through in seam allowances or facings, and color should not be altered. Sheer Blender® and Sheer Fuse™ interfacings are specifically designed to prevent shadow-through of prints and to blend with colors of sheer fashion fabrics. These interfacings are available in several colors and should be selected to blend with the background color of printed fabrics.

Textures and fabric stretch, or give, should be retained. A crinkled surface should not be flattened by the application of a fusible interfacing. Stretchable fabrics require an interfacing that also stretches if that characteristic is to be retained.

Fiber content and fabric finish may repel fusing adhesives or prohibit high temperatures necessary for fusing. Any fabric with a water-resistant or soil-repellant finish will resist fusible application. In that case, fusibles may be applied to a sew-in interfacing to add crispness. The interfacing should be compatible with the care requirements of the fabric, especially launderability.

The design of the garment influences whether you should use interfacing. For example, there would be no reason to interface a blouson bodice facing or a tie neck. If the fabric or design doesn't need interfacing, you can eliminate it in a major area while adding small amounts for details, such as buttonholes. The areas to be interfaced may vary in the amount of firmness desired. Collar points may require a second layer of fusible interfacing. The flexibility of the collar is maintained while adding crispness to the point only. The collar and cuffs may be firmer than the bodice facing. The design of the garment will be the determining factor.

Garment Construction

The construction of the garment may help you select the interfacing. The type of construction may indicate whether a fusible or a sew-in interfacing should be used. Examination of ready-to-wear will show that the interfacing is always placed under the outer or top layer of fabric to prevent the shadowing of seam allowances and to give a smoother result. Preventing the shadowing of seam allowances should be the main consideration. It is especially important if the fabric has some transparency or is a smooth-surfaced solid color.

A fold-over attached facing may be safely interfaced with a fusible on the facing side. Because a separate facing requires a seam, the interfacing should be applied to the garment, rather than to the facing, to prevent shadowing. If the interfacing is fusible, it should continue to the side seam to prevent a ridge.

The controversy over sew-in versus fusible interfacing continues and seems to be directly related to the method learned by the individual sewer. The desired result should help the sewer make a choice. Don't overlook the possibility of using both methods in one garment. Sew-in interfacings can be basted to the layer to which they are to be applied. The basting can be done by hand, machine, or glue stick.

Self-fabric interfacing should not be overlooked as a possible sew-in for sheer and lightweight fabrics. The color always matches, and the original fabric drape will be easily preserved.

Flexibility

Certain areas, such as rolled collars and French cuffs, require flexibility in order to roll smoothly. These areas are best interfaced with an all-bias non-woven or a woven cut on the bias grain, probably a sew-in. Each area requires a two-way flexibility, as it must bend or curve around the body as well as over another part of the garment, whereas a plain cuff or collar stand will bend only around the body.

Hair canvas belongs in a category all to itself. It is the traditional interfacing for suits and coats constructed of firmly woven wool and blends. It gives a firm, crisp structure to the garment. Hair canvases are a combination of cotton, rayon, polyester, and goat hair. A higher percentage of goat hair is an indication of better quality. Thread count is also a factor. A lower thread count, which results in a looser weave, lends itself nicely to shaping; a higher thread count, which is tightly woven, is easier to handle.

Except for Acro, which is also available as a fusible, hair canvases are sew-ins and drycleanable only. Hair canvas is inherently firm and crisp, so the additional weight added by fusing may not be necessary. Because the texture of hair canvas allows it to cling to the fashion fabric, application of a sew-in is an easy matter.

Testing Interfacing

Always check an interfacing, either by draping the fabric and a sew-in over your hand to duplicate the look you want in your garment or by fusing a sample.

You may want to purchase ¼ yard (.25 m) of several fusibles to have on hand for testing purposes with each fashion fabric you use. Purchasing small amounts of interfacings is also a good way to test new products. Periodically review the interfacing inventory in stores to search for new ones. You may wish to save time and money by stockpiling several interfacings that will work with most of your sewing.

Most interfacings say "preshrunk," but experience shows that it is best to do your own preshrinking. Place the folded interfacing in hot water, and allow it to soak for about fifteen minutes. Then remove it, and allow it to drain on a folded bath towel. When most of the water is drained, open and lay the interfacing as a single layer on carpeting or a towel so it can air dry. Label and fold it loosely until needed.

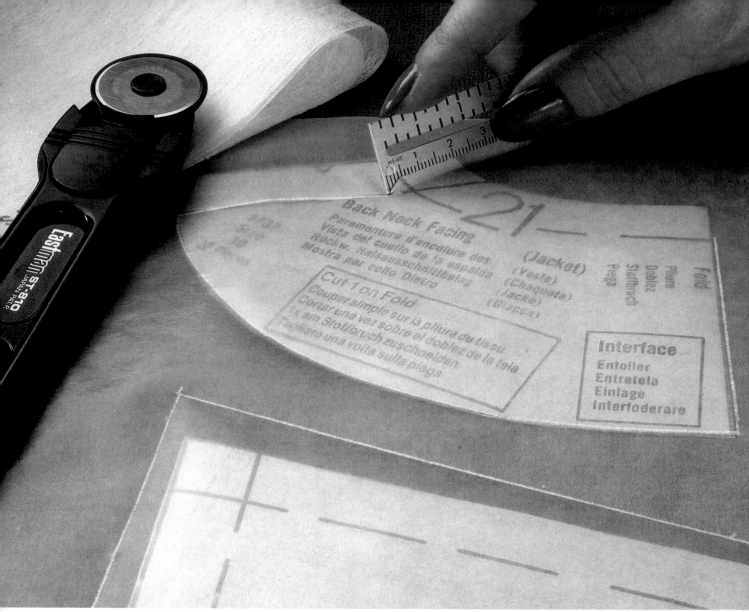

There are two quick and easy methods to cut out fusible interfacings and eliminate seam allowances without destroying the pattern. Lay wax paper on the pattern and trace with the tip of a seam gauge, eliminating seam allowances. If the interfacing is transparent, simply lay it on top of the pattern, and trace with a marking pen on the stitching line; cut out with a rotary cutter.

To test a fusible interfacing, use a 6" (15 cm) square of fashion fabric and a 3" by 6" (7.5 by 15 cm) piece of interfacing. Place the interfacing on half the fabric. Fuse as directed, using the manufacturer's recommended temperature, time, and pressure. Turn over and press from the right side to draw the adhesive into the fabric for better bonding.

Then, even though the fashion fabric and the interfacing may have been preshrunk, reshrink the fused swatch. Bubbles will be an indication of differential shrinkage. If bubbles appear on the fabric side, the interfacing has shrunk. If they appear on the interfacing side, the fabric has shrunk. Some fabrics, particularly cotton, have residual shrinkage and will continue to shrink through several launderings.

Sufficient heat, time, and pressure are the three important factors involved. Too much heat or the use of a reflective ironing board cover, which tends to increase the heat applied, might shrink certain synthetic interfacings, such as nylon knits, during the fusing process. Time and heat are frequently stressed, but sufficient pressure is also important. Lowering the ironing board slightly to gain leverage may help.

Keep a record of the fashion fabric, fiber content, interfacing, any special fusing techniques, and comments. Also save any trial fusing swatches. This will be helpful in future selection of interfacing. There will be times when you'll be surprised that such a thin layer of interfacing can add so much crispness to the fabric, whereas others tend to add more bulk.

The chart on the opposite page suggests interfacings that have proved satisfactory through testing and actual use. Some appear in more than one category because they perform well with a range of fabric weights and uses. Experiment with different interfacings; it is what is behind the fashion fabric that makes an excellent finished garment.

Guide to Interfacings

	Interfacing Weight	Fabric	Interfacing	Sew-in or Fusible	Special Data
Separates & Dresses	**Sheer**	Voile, chiffon, gauze, batiste, leno, georgette, crepe de chine, charmeuse, lace, silk broadcloth	Self-fabric	S	Matches color and "hand"
			Sheer Sew-In™	S	Nonwoven
			Sheerweight #905	S	Nonwoven
			*Organza	S	Variety of colors
	Soft	Challis, jersey, tricot, polyester & silk crepe, tissue faille	*Easy-Knit®	F	Knit, white, beige, black, gray
			*KnitShape®	F	Knit, white, natural, black
			Self-fabric	S	Matches color and "hand"
			Sheer Blenders®	F	Nonwoven, white, beige, charcoal
			So-Sheer™	F	Nonwoven, white, beige, charcoal
			Sheer Fuse™	F	Nonwoven, white, light charcoal, print blender
	Crisp	Shirtings, gingham, poplin, chambray, seersucker, cotton & cotton blend broadcloth, oxford cloth, piqué, lightweight linen, pincord, lightweight denim, madras	Shirt-Fuse®	F	Nonwoven
			*Pellon® #911	F	All bias, white, gray
			Self-fabric	S	Matches color and "hand"
			*Armo Press® Soft	S	Woven, permanent press
			Shape-Flex® All Purpose	S	Woven
			ShirTailor®	F	Nonwoven, white, charcoal
Coats, Dresses, Jackets & Suits	**Soft**	wool & wool-like crepe, linen types, poplin, duck, chino, cotton & cotton blend twills, faille, denim, noil, velveteen, velvet	Armo Press® Soft	S	Woven, permanent press
			*Whisper Weft	F	Weft, white, gray, beige
			Shape-Flex® All Purpose	S	Woven
			*Sof-Shape®	F	All bias, white, charcoal
			KnitShape®	F	Knit, white, natural, black
			Easy-Knit®	F	Knit, white, beige, black, gray
	Crisp	Linen types, poplin, denim, wool & wool blends, flannel, gabardine, mohair, synthetic suedes & leather, coatings, corduroy	*Armo Press® Firm	S	Woven, permanent press
			*Armo® Weft	F	Weft, white, gray, beige, black
			*Pel Aire®	F	Nonwoven, natural, charcoal
			*Suit-Shape®	F	Weft, white, gray
			Sewers' Choice™	S	Hair canvas, dryclean only
			Hair Canvas #77	S	Dryclean only
			Acro Hair Canvas	S	Machine washable
		Rainwear	Pellon® #930	S	Nonwoven, all bias
			Veriform® Durable Press	S	Woven, permanent press
			Armo Press® Firm	S	Woven, permanent press
		Fur, fake fur, fleece	Sewers' Choice™	S	Hair canvas, dryclean only
			Hair Canvas #77	S	Dryclean only
			Armo Press® Firm	S	Woven permanent press
			Sta-Shape® Durable Press	S	Woven, permanent press
Stretch Fabrics	**Soft**	T-shirt knits, jerseys, lightweight sweater knits	SRF™	F	Nonwoven, white, charcoal
			KnitShape®	F	Knit, white, natural, black
			Easy-Knit®	F	Knit, white, beige, black, gray
			Soft-Fuse™	F	Nonwoven
			Stretch-Ease™	F	Nonwoven, white, charcoal
	Firm	Double knits, terry, velour, sweatshirt fleece, stretch poplin & denim, heavy sweater knits	Uni-Stretch®	F	Nonwoven
			Tailor's Touch®	F	Nonwoven
			Mid-Heavy Weight #931	F	Stretches across, stable in length

*Stockpile suggestions

Types of Interfacings

1) Polyester fleece is available in many varieties and is useful in shoulder pads and trapunto trims as well as for crafts.

2) Waistband interfacings are both specific and general. Fusibles made specifically for waistbands are Waist Shaper® and Fold-a-Band™. Waist Shaper is firmer and has no seam allowances. The sew-ins that are best known are Ban-Rol and Armoflexxx®. Both are non-roll and do not include seam allowances; fasten to the waistband seam either before or after the band is applied to the garment. Ban-Rol is available as an elastic and as a stable product with a coated edge. Its shrinkage is negligible. Armoflexxx shrinks considerably and has no finish on the edges; it can be contoured to fit a shaped waistband (page 74). Rol-Control™, a new product on the market, has one seam allowance; it is flexible in length, yet it does not roll. The one seam allowance with a stitching guide allows for easy application. In general, any firm interfacing such as

Acro or a nonwoven stabilizer can be used if desired, but will tend to roll in time.

3) Slotted interfacings, such as Fold-a-Band, come as one-slot and two-slot for hems and facings.

4) Special-purpose fusible interfacings, such as Quilter's Secret™, are fused to the wrong side of fabric before cutting. Quilter's Secret has cutting and stitching lines so that in addition to supporting the fabric and stopping raveling or fraying, it makes sewing straight seams and matching corners easier and quicker.

5) Stabilizers, such as Tear-Away, Trace Erase, Trace Erase Grid, and Stitch-n-Tear®, can be used under buttonholes and decorative stitchwork to stabilize fabric. Remove stabilizer when stitching is completed. Solvey, Stitch-n-Spray™, and Wash-Away are water-soluble plastic stabilizers. Because the stabilizer completely dissolves with the addition of water, no white remnants remain embedded in the stitches.

6) Fusible webs are excellent timesaving products for hems, appliqués, trims, and basting. Although not an interfacing product, fusible web adds weight and stiffness. Stitch Witchery® and Wonder-Web™ are used for fusing fabric to fabric. Perky Bond® is a similar product. Fine Fuse™ is soft and ultralight and desirable for hemming with soft, drapable fabrics such as knits. Wonder-Under™ transfer fusing web and Transfuse™ II are paper-backed fusible webs. They quickly turn any fabric into a fusible fabric. The paper backing acts as a release sheet. Draw shapes onto paper backing, and cut out before or after fusing.

7) Release sheets, such as Transfuse, are reusable nonstick sheets that can be used with the fusible webs for fabric-to-fabric fusing. Fusible web is placed on the wrong side of the fabric and covered with the release sheet. The iron comes in contact with the release sheet only. It allows precise placement, because you can see what you are doing. Transfuse also protects the iron soleplate from sticky residue. A second step is required to fuse the now fusible fabric in position.

8) Special-purpose nonwoven material, such as Enlarge-a-Design and Tru-Grid®, can be used to make fitting shells in addition to enlarging designs for appliqué, quilting, and crafts.

9) Tracing webs, such as Trace-a-Pattern, Pattern Tracer, and Do Sew, are useful for copying paper patterns from ready-to-wear because they are strong, flexible, and transparent. They can be pinned to a garment and cut along the seamlines, which are visible through the pattern tracing material.

Margaret Deck Komives teaches all levels of clothing construction at Milwaukee Area Technical College, North Campus. She and her students have used and tested the products mentioned in the article.

Unraveling the Mysteries of Thread

by Carol Neumann

Sewing decisions used to be so simple: calico for a dress, wool for a coat, and size 50 cotton thread for both. A population explosion of thread fibers and types has occurred to keep up with the technological expansion of fabrics. As a result, no one thread will satisfy all sewing needs.

Thread is a basic notion often taken for granted, but it can have a tremendous influence on sewing success. Select thread according to the fabric weight and fiber content; the machine being used, conventional or serger; and the end use, construction or embellishment.

All-purpose Threads

All-purpose threads are those that may be used for several purposes on a wide variety of fabrics, and on both conventional machines and sergers. They are usually three-ply threads but may also be two-ply. Each ply is made of several fibers that are twisted together to form one thread.

Cotton-wrapped polyester is the most common all-purpose thread. Each ply is a polyester core wrapped with cotton. The cotton provides excellent sewability, smoothness, and luster. The polyester core provides strength and elasticity for the thread to stretch with the fabric. A general-purpose weight is used for most fabrics; however, a heavy-duty version can be used for extra-heavy fabrics, where strength is a necessity. Cotton-wrapped polyester is glazed for ease of use on all fabrics but especially multilayered, heavy fabrics.

Polyester thread is strong and abrasion resistant, and it stretches and recovers with the fabric. It may be a *short-staple* thread, where polyester filaments are cut into 1½" (3.8 cm) lengths and then spun into thread. Because of the short lengths, it is fuzzy and may produce lint, which collects in the machine. *Long-staple* polyester begins with 4" to 5" (10 to 12.5 cm) filaments that are spun into thread. Long-staple polyester thread is finer, smoother, and more even than the short-staple. Jet texturing and a spun process are other methods that produce softer thread while retaining the original strength.

Specialty Threads

Specialty threads are those that are designed for use on one kind of fabric or for one purpose. Machine specialty threads may be used in the serger as well as a conventional sewing machine. Try a regular serger thread, or a semitransparent polyester or nylon transparent, in the needles and specialty threads in the loopers. Loopers will readily accept lightweight yarns and lightweight, supple ribbons. Adjust tension and stitch length and width to experiment with these threads.

Button and carpet thread is a tough, thick cotton-wrapped polyester thread for hand sewing. It is perfect for making and mending carpets and rugs and for sewing buttons, snaps, or hooks and eyes onto coats and jackets.

Cotton thread is strong with very limited elasticity. It should be used on natural fibers that have a limited amount of give, such as light to heavyweight linen and cotton. Mercerized cotton thread has been treated to make it lustrous and absorbent to dyes.

Cotton basting thread is fine to prevent indentations after the stitching is pressed. It breaks easily for quick removal of basting. For decorative work, cotton basting thread is recommended for use in the bobbin when a machine embroidery thread is the top thread.

Machine embroidery thread is available as cotton and cotton-wrapped polyester. A fine 60 weight cotton is used for embroidery, monogramming, and French hand sewing, as well as for fine, lightweight fabrics. Because of the thickness, the heavier 30 weight cotton is best used for satin stitching when a faster fill is desired.

Metallic threads are shiny synthetic threads used for machine embroidery and decorative stitching. Make sure the thread is nontarnishing, washable, and dry-cleanable. Add sparkle to a silk scarf or a holiday napkin with a rolled hem done in a combination of metallics and regular thread.

Nylon thread is a monofilament, transparent thread available in a fine and medium weight. The medium weight is not recommended for garments because it is stiff, wiry, and uncomfortable next to the skin. Both weights will melt at high temperatures, so they are best used on projects that will not need much ironing. The finer weight is useful for blind hemming on garments of any color, because it is available in clear for light colors, and smoke-color for darker colors. Because it blends with all colors, drapery makers prefer it. Continuous use of nylon thread can wear needles and the loopers on sergers. Needles are inexpensive to replace, but loopers are a costly item.

Nylon thread has many applications on the serger. Use in the lower looper in conjunction with a yarn or ribbon in the upper looper; only the yarn or ribbon will show. On a wedding veil, try a narrow rolled hem with nylon thread. This thread gives the hem weight and stiffness for a wonderful rippled edge. Nylon thread is available on spools and cones.

Quilting thread is available as all cotton or cotton-wrapped polyester. It is designed for hand stitching or machine sewing. It is strong and has a finish that aids sewing through layers of fabrics and fiberfill. The cotton is recommended for natural fibers.

Woolly nylon is a texturized form of nylon that is applicable for garments. Woolly nylon is soft and stretchy. It is particularly good for lingerie, swimwear, and activewear.

Woolly nylon was originally made for the serger. Use it in loopers and needles, or in loopers only. For all activewear and swimwear, be sure to use it in both needles and loopers for maximum stretchability of seams during wear. Woolly nylon fills in rapidly and makes an attractive rolled hem on napkins. This yarn-like thread is difficult to thread; a needle threader and a *serger looper and needle threader* are helpful.

Rayon thread is shiny, silky, and beautiful for decorative stitching. A 40 weight is fine and suitable for monogramming and embroidery. The 30 weight is heavier and best for machine satin stitching, because it fills in faster and fuller than the 40 weight. A thread net is a handy notion that will keep this slippery thread on the tube and tangle-free.

Silk thread is strong and lustrous with good elasticity. It can be used on most fabrics, but the cost is prohibitive. Silk is usually reserved for a decorative effect, such as topstitching or machine embroidery.

Topstitching and **buttonhole twist** thread are similar in weight and use. As their names imply, they are used for topstitching and sewing on buttons. They may be made of cotton-wrapped polyester, polyester, or silk. Because of the thickness of these threads, they can be difficult to use. A special topstitching needle or a size 16 (100) or larger is an absolute necessity. Avoid backstitching because the heavy thread quickly piles up. If problems occur, use a straight-stitch needle plate, or cover the needle hole with a piece of tape. The needle will pierce a single hole. Use an all-purpose thread or cotton basting thread on the bobbin. If all else fails, wind the topstitching thread on the bobbin and use an all-purpose thread on the top. Stitching from the wrong side will be necessary.

Topstitching/buttonhole thread is now available on a 328-yard (312 m) crosswound spool, which makes it convenient and economical for serger use.

Water-soluble thread is a new item in the world of thread. It is soluble in water, but not in drycleaning solution. Dissolve this thread by laundering or sponging with a wet cloth; or cover with a wet press cloth, and steam. The cloth will absorb the thread residue. It is necessary to use water-soluble thread as a top thread only, because the bottom thread will fall away when the soluble thread is dissolved. Use it for any temporary stitching. Keep your hands dry during use, and store water-soluble thread in an airtight plastic bag to protect it from humidity, which will soften the fiber. Softened thread will become gummy and will be useless.

Yarns, pearl and **crochet cotton**, and **narrow ribbon** are examples of embellishment threads. Although they won't fit through the needle of a sewing machine, they can be couched in place by hand or with the use of a blindstitch on the sewing machine.

When yarn, pearl cotton, and topstitching thread are used on a serger, they make heavy, braidlike edgings; or they can be used in a flatlock seam on the outside of a garment. Number 5 pearl cotton is now also available on a 150-yard (143 m) cone in ten colors. It has a special finish that makes it easier to use in a serger. Silk or synthetic silk ribbon, $\frac{1}{16}$" or $\frac{1}{8}$" (1.5 or 3 mm) wide, can be used to create a braid look on boiled wool.

Serger Thread

All-purpose thread can be used on the serger, but there are better alternatives. Sergers use a lot of thread because of stitch configuration and because they use from two to five threads. Conventional sewing machine spools come in several sizes, containing 120 to 1094 yards (110 to 1000 m). When all-purpose thread is used on the serger, thread is used up quickly. Serger thread, in contrast, is wound on several sizes of cones and tubes, from 1000 to 6000 yards (950 to 5700 m) to give the consumer greater yardage.

It is difficult to estimate how much thread is needed to serge one garment, but for specialty threads such as yarns and pearl cotton, plan to use five to six times the stitching length plus extra for experimentation and testing.

Because sergers use two or more threads in combination, finer, softer thread is required. Stiff and wiry threads pop out of thread guides and can cause skipped stitches. For this reason, serger threads are two-ply and a finer weight than all-purpose thread.

Cotton-wrapped polyester is the most common serger thread. It has the same characteristics as the all-purpose cotton-wrapped polyester, except it is two-ply and crosswound on a cone. The mercerized cotton is lustrous and readily accepts dye. The polyester core is strong and, most important, elastic.

Polyester thread is also two-ply and comes as spun poly or the poly-wrapped poly, which is a poly

core with a spun poly wrap. Testing has shown that the poly-wrapped poly is stronger than the spun poly alone.

Thread weight may be indicated by a number such as 60/2; the second number refers to the ply. A weight of 60 or above is preferable. The most recommended weights are 70 and 100. A fine thread does not mean less strength; the thread fiber and the way it is manufactured have a lot to do with strength. When extra strength is needed, a three-ply serger thread is available on cones.

Serger thread may also be used on conventional sewing machines. Although the thread is two-ply, it is extremely strong and suitable for all except the heaviest of fabrics where strength is an absolute necessity. A cone thread stand will allow cones to be used with a conventional sewing machine.

Good-quality thread is always important but even more so with a serger. Because of the number of threads, the complex threading, and the manner in

Left to right: Yarn, rayon, and variegated thread are used in the upper looper of a serger for attractive edge finishes.

which the threads are combined, the thread must flow smoothly and evenly from the cone. To facilitate a smooth flow from the cone, serger thread is always crosswound. Looping the thread diagonally up and down the cone gives the longest distance with the least curve and allows for a tangle-free flow when you are sewing at the high speeds of sergers. Examine thread for smoothness, uniform diameter, and fuzziness. Lint can really gum up a serger.

Color of Thread

Thread colors are updated seasonally to reflect fashion fabrics. Up to 250 colors are available in the all-purpose thread for conventional sewing machines. Serger threads are available in up to fourteen basic colors.

Select construction thread that matches the fabric or that is one shade darker. Choose the predominant color for plaids, tweeds, or prints. For serger threads, keep basics such as white, khaki, black, navy, and gray on hand. They will blend with most colors. If a closer

match is needed, the needle thread should match the fabric because it is the only thread that might show from the right side. Semitransparent serger thread comes in twelve colors that blend to match the fabric. Variegated threads make interesting color banding, and can be used on either type of machine.

Sources:
Catherine's of Lexington, Rte. 6, Box 1227, Lexington, NC 27292. *Clotilde, Inc.*, 237 SW 28th St., Fort Lauderdale, FL 33315. *Herrschners, Inc.*, Hoover Rd., Stevens Point, WI 54492. *Nancy's Notions*®, Box 683, Beaver Dam, WI 53916. *Speed Stitch*, Box 3472, Port Charlotte, FL 33952. *Treadleart*, 25834 Narbonne Ave., Lomita, CA 90717. *YLI Corporation*, 45 West 300 North, Provo, UT 84601.

Carol Neumann is a staff member of the Singer Sewing Reference Library with experience in sewing, education, and retail fabric sales.

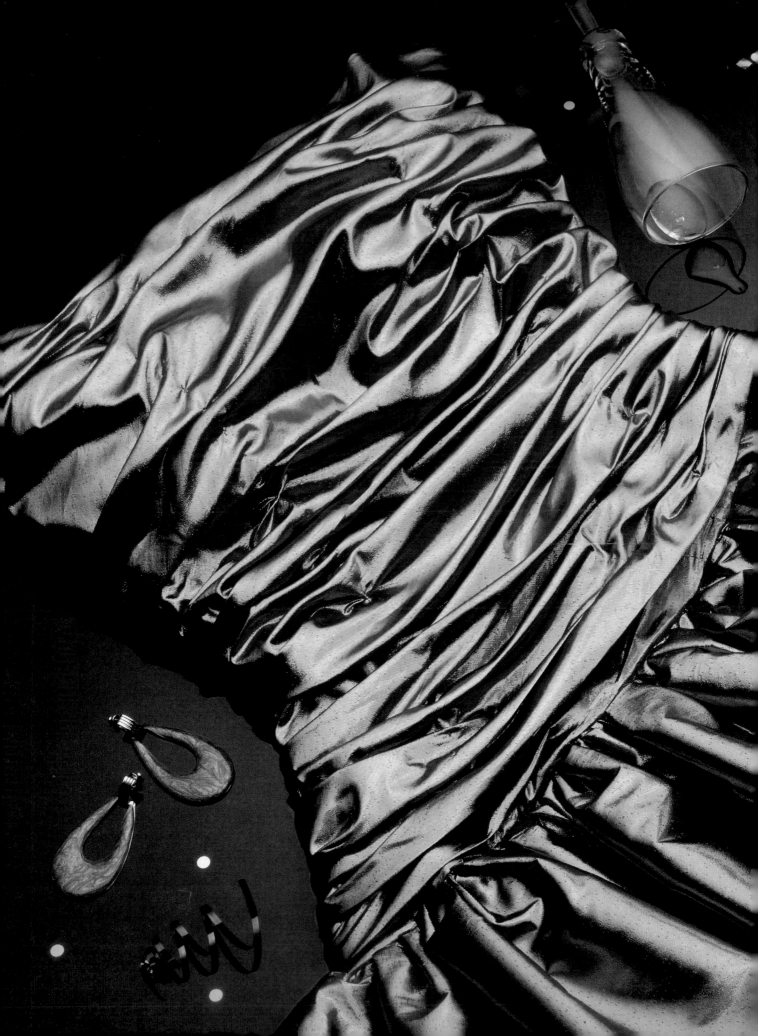

Wearable Fashions

Shaping Up Your Wardrobe for the Coming Season

by Anne Marie Soto

Is your wardrobe suffering from a case of the blahs? Are your closets and drawers filled with clothes that are out of date, inappropriate for your current lifestyle, or unflattering to your figure? Are you always sewing against a deadline because you've got nothing suitable for that special occasion? If any of this sounds like you, now is the time to get your wardrobe in shape. The dilemma is how to go about it and where to find the time.

Analyzing Your Lifestyle

When it comes to clothing, many of us have fallen into bad buying habits. We buy and sew the same type of clothes year after year, regardless of how our lifestyle has changed. For example, a person promoted to manager may still dress casually, even though an executive look would be more appropriate. Years of wearing the washable garments that mothers of young children find so practical may have blinded our eyes to the joys of sewing on fine, dryclean-only fabrics.

It is likely that your lifestyle has changed somewhat over the last few years. Has your wardrobe kept pace? Perhaps now is the time to introduce some more sophisticated items or to trade in that tailored wardrobe for styles that are softer or more casual.

Analyzing Your Fashion Personality

When it comes to getting your wardrobe in shape, your fashion personality is as important a consideration as your lifestyle. There are three basic approaches to dressing. One of them will sound like the real you.

• Tailored dressing includes simple, uncluttered clothes with classic lines, small geometric prints, stripes, checks, foulards, and basic colors.

• Romantic dressing relies on softer colors, small floral prints, and lace touches.

• Dramatic dressing uses strong colors, ethnic prints, and unusual jewelry.

Any outfit, from business suit to bathing suit, can reflect your fashion personality. The challenge is to avoid settling for something that's less-than-you. The "dress for success" suit may look severe and unfriendly on you unless you soften it with a lace-trimmed blouse and pearls or dramatize it with a bright sweater and art deco lapel pins.

The fabric that's on sale for a great price may not look so wonderful on you. Like most of us, you've probably got several of these bargains in your stash of fabric. Don't compound your mistakes by sewing them. Instead, gather a few friends and organize a fabric swap (one woman's "trash" is another woman's perfect color), or be a sport and donate it to a charity with a sewing program.

Learning from Experience

Books and articles about wardrobe planning often recommend a system of analyzing your wardrobe through extensive inventory charts and a daily activities diary. These systems work fine if you have the time. The truth is that most of us have the good intentions, but not the follow-through. Somehow, we never quite find that rainy afternoon to try everything on. Or after a day or two of faithfully recording what we wore when, we get bored.

Here's an easier method to get you started. Clear out a section of your closet. Then, for the next three weeks, every time you finish wearing something, hang it in that section. You may find that over the three-week period, you're constantly adding garments to the section. Or you may find that, for the second and third week, you're wearing essentially the same things you wore the first week.

At the end of this time period, you will have identified your collection of core clothes. These are the garments that make up the heart of your wardrobe. If you're like most people, only about 10 percent of your wardrobe will end up in this group. The other 90 percent is hardly ever worn.

If you wear an item of clothing regularly, it has something going for it. One of the keys to getting your wardrobe in shape is to identify these positive traits. Then you can consciously use this knowledge to plan future sewing projects.

Now, it's time for some simplified recording and analysis. Using the chart that follows as your model, develop one of your own. In the left-hand column, write a brief description of each core garment. Then, working across the remaining columns, put check marks under all the traits that apply.

Once your chart is completed, the next step is to analyze what those check marks tell you about the strengths and weaknesses of your wardrobe. For example, in the chart you may have a lot of marks under "Feels Comfortable" but very few under "Gets Compliments." This tells you that you need to make your wardrobe visually more exciting. You may have a lot of marks under "Coordinates with Other Items" but very few under "Color Is Flattering." While it's obvious that you know how to plan a wardrobe, you need to learn to be more adventurous about color.

Now go back to the garments, and take a second look. What are the flattering colors? Why are some garments so comfortable? How do they create the body illusion you desire? If you can apply these answers to future sewing projects, the happy result will be a more satisfying wardrobe.

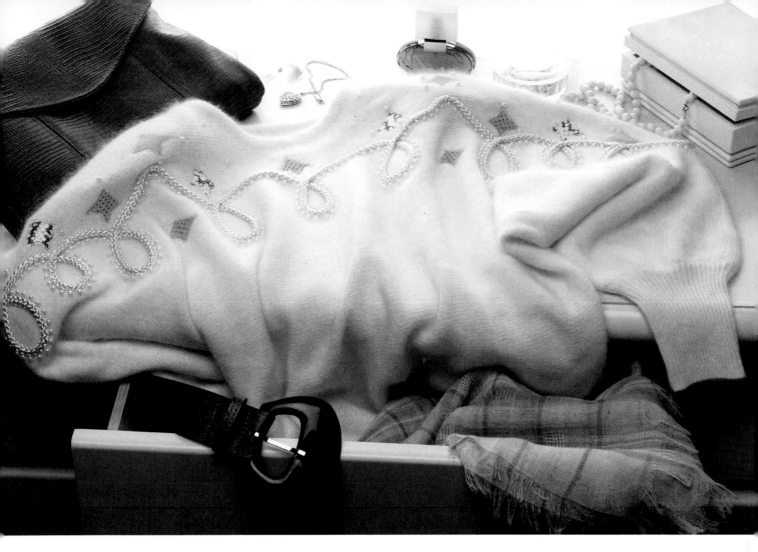

Wardrobe Analysis

Item	feels comfortable	fits well	gets compliments	color is flattering	coordinates with other items	camouflages body
black gabardine pants	✓				✓	✓
cream silk blouse	✓			✓	✓	
red cardigan – wool itches			✓	✓	difficult to match	✓
brown plaid skirt	✓		✓			

A Wardrobe That Works

The successful wardrobe is a versatile wardrobe, one that's composed of individual pieces that work together to form an integrated whole. This doesn't necessitate a closet full of clothes. The way to get a lot of wardrobe out of just a few garments is to follow some simple planning strategies.

A wardrobe should be built around two or three basic colors, ones that complement each other and flatter the wearer. Choose one color to serve as your primary basic; the other two will be your secondary colors. Your primary color could be a standard neutral, such as black, navy, gray, or brown, or something a bit more unusual, such as burgundy, red, camel, hunter green, or teal. Your goal is to develop a collection of separates built around this color. Plan to introduce gradually to your wardrobe a skirt, tailored jacket, pants, turtleneck or other pullover sweater, and a sweater jacket in this primary color. Use the secondary colors for blouses and additional tops.

If your lifestyle is more formal, the skirt, tailored jacket, and pants should all be of the same fabric so that they can be worn as a matched suit. If your lifestyle is more casual, consider mixing solids, tweeds, and plaids. Once you've acquired the basics, add additional pieces from both your primary and your secondary colors.

It's essential that your primary and secondary colors be ones that are flattering and that you enjoy wearing. If you're unsure what colors are best for you, consider enlisting the services of a color consultant. Although there are several systems of color analysis, the results depend as much on the individual color consultant as on the system. The best color consultants are partly born and partly made, a combination of innate talent and learned skills. To determine whether this is the color consultant for you, ask for the names of some previous clients; then talk with them. Find out how long ago they consulted with this person about their colors, if they followed the system, and how satisfied they were with the results.

A Classic, Trend, or Fad

A workable wardrobe is one that has the right balance of classic designs and new styles. Just what that balance is depends a great deal on whether you function in a conservative or a flamboyant environment and how long you want your clothes to last.

A classic is a traditional style that will stay in fashion a long time. It includes pleated trousers, a blazer jacket, and an A-line skirt. A trend is a slow change in a specific style or a certain way of wearing clothes. Shorter skirts, shoulder pads, and fashion designer Donna Karan's concept of body dressing are examples of current trends. A fad is a fashion that comes and goes almost overnight. Spotting a fad can be tricky because it sometimes masquerades as a trend. For example, the enormously oversized look that Japanese designers introduced several seasons ago appeared to be a trend. However, since it virtually disappeared within a season, it turned out to be a fad.

The best way to make sure you won't be stuck with a lot of expensive fads in your wardrobe is to follow two simple rules. First, try out a new look with relatively inexpensive items, preferably accessories, that won't tie up your money or your sewing time. Second, put the larger items on next season's sewing agenda. If they are still around at that time, you can sew with the confidence that it's a trend you're looking at and not a flash-in-the-pan fad.

Expanding Your Wardrobe

One of the best strategies for expanding your wardrobe is to choose seasonless fabrics. These fabrics will be appropriate for all but the very hottest or coldest days of the year. Rayon, silk, cotton, crepe, lightweight wool gabardine, denim, challis, taffeta, and many knits can look fashionable year round.

Once you find a pattern that looks great and fits well, why not use it to full advantage? Consider using the same pattern to make your winter coat and your raincoat. Sew the same pants pattern in worsted wool and casual corduroy; the same jacket, in linen and in tweed. Not only will you save money on patterns, you'll save sewing time, too. The second version will sew twice as fast as the first.

Another way to get more mileage out of your wardrobe is to choose separates that can do multiple duty. For example, two-piece dresses can split up into skirts and blouses, a matching pants and shirt can masquerade as a jumpsuit, blouses extended to below-the-hip lengths can double as tunics or belted overshirts, and winter shirts can be worn as summer jackets.

Separates do multiple duty. A blouse can be worn with coordinating pants or with a matching skirt to give the look of a one-piece dress.

Today's Fashion: Where Is It Headed?

No one has a crystal ball to predict fashions. However, there are some trends you should keep in mind to help you revamp and update your wardrobe in the coming seasons.

The trend is toward a simplified style of dressing without excessive ornamentation. It's best exemplified in body-conscious knits, draped and wrapped silhouettes, and small details that stand out. These touches include novelty trims, such as soutache braid, frogs, and tassels. The watchword well into 1989 is quality. Being expensive isn't as important as looking expensive, so this is the perfect time to shape up your wardrobe.

A minimal color scheme of black and white starts strong in spring '88 and continues as ebony and ivory (think piano keys) for fall. Look for minimal color in spring and summer in solids and prints. In the fall, you'll also find it introduced in the weave of the fabric, à la menswear stripes, tweeds, diagonals, and plaids.

Aristocratic influences of English gentry, country French, and Italian Renaissance show up in fabrics. Think velvets, tweeds, plaids, herringbones, paisleys, and small pattern mixings.

Blackened darks for fall '88 can be worn together or with black and pastels. Look for deep greens, burgundies, and blues. The blackened darks are particularly good in prints such as dark prints on darker backgrounds.

Men's suiting influences career dressing in flat wools, crepes, and gabardines.

Shorter hemlines continue, particularly on straight skirts. Be watchful of the word *mini*. It can mean anything from covering the knee to mid-knee to above-the-knee. Soft, full skirts will still look best below the knee and will often be mated to shorter tops.

Fur appears on collars, cuffs, and as boas for winter suits and coats.

Exaggerated shoulders and hips give the newest suits and dresses a decidedly hourglass shape.

Anne Marie Soto, nationally known expert in the field of fashion sewing, is the author of numerous articles and publications, including Vogue's Sewing for Your Children.

The Glamour Girls Are Back

by Barbara Weiland O'Connell

Just when you began to tire of padded shoulders and shapeless, oversized fashion, designers offered the first hints of more feminine fit and flare. The return to body-conscious dressing made way for this year's grand-entrance glamour looks, fashion nostalgia we haven't seen or worn since the '40s and '50s. With fitted waistlines again in style, full-skirted designs reminiscent of bouffant Marilyn Monroe crinolines — plus a blitz of bubbles, flounces, and poufs — emphasize a curvy, hourglass shape that clearly announces "the woman is back."

Bustiers, body-hugging bodices, off-shoulder looks, and long-torso designs prevail in evening and bridal designs. Dart-fitting and shaped seams sculpt stiffer dressy fabrics like taffeta, satin, and peau de soie to fit soft, feminine curves. Crisp nylon net, organza, tulle, and dotted point d'esprit create the fullness and pouf under fanciful, romantic skirts that run the gamut from provocatively short and full or fitted, to shaped or draped, to full sweeps in ballerina and floor-length ballgowns.

Perfect the Fit

With fullness concentrated in the skirt, glamour dressing for 1988 relies on a close-to-the-body fit on top, and that means brushing up on sewing-to-fit skills. Tissue-fitting the bodice before cutting can give you an idea of how the pattern will fit. But because glamour fabrics readily show needle marks and stitching lines, it may be a time and money-saver to cut and sew a trial bodice from a lightweight nonwoven interfacing. Use it to fine-tune the fit, then as the actual pattern when cutting from fashion fabric. If only minor fitting adjustments are necessary, shortcut the trial bodice by fitting the bodice lining first; then transfer changes to the fashion fabric.

Strapless and off-shoulder styles rely on an inner superstructure for stay-put power. New lightweight featherboning provides the shaping. Strips of grosgrain ribbon stitched to the seams and darts of the bodice lining create the casing to hold the boning in place. For comfort's sake, round the ends of the boning with sharp scissors before slipping it into the casing. If the cut edges are especially rough, file them smooth with an emery board or nail file.

Zippers are also key to fitted bodice fashion. Use your favorite method of insertion, lapped or centered, and try the hand-picked variety for a special couture touch and almost hidden stitches. To relieve strain on the zipper at the waistline as well as help support the weight of full skirts, add a grosgrain ribbon stay to fitted waistlines. Cut a strip of ½" to 1" (1.3 to 2.5 cm) wide grosgrain ribbon to fit the waistline of the completed dress, adding 1" (2.5 cm) for finishing the ends. Turn the ends under ½" (1.3 cm), and stitch; then sew hooks and eyes to the ends, with the loops extending over the edge. Hand-tack the stay to seams and darts.

Youthful full-skirted silhouettes rely on inner support achieved with crisp fabrics used as petticoats or underlining. For added shaping and away-from-the body fullness, sew nylon horsehair braid to the bottom edge of crinoline petticoats or the actual skirt ruffles and flounces. Stitch to the lower edge at the hemline on the outside; then turn to the inside, and edgestitch through all layers.

Glamorous Options

If understated elegance is your glamour style, there are several looks in evening separates on the fashion menu. Wear a sweater long and low over a skirt with hemline flare. Or try the unexpected. Make a short black lace skirt to team with a cashmere sweater set in pale pink. Hand-tack matching lace trim just above the bottom ribbing of the pullover and on the sleeves of the cardigan.

Add a touch of shine to a pretty printed chiffon or georgette print by outlining a predominant design motif with strings of tiny beads, rhinestones, or sequins. Hold in position with glue stick; then hand-tack loosely in place.

When it comes to all-out glamour-girl dressing, we haven't had so many alluring and feminine choices in years. From ingenue looks in froufrou crinolines and bubble skirts to more sophisticated, shoulder-baring ballgowns and short-skirted cancan dresses, these dress-up styles ensure some unforgettable romantic evenings.

Barbara Weiland O'Connell is a nationally known sewing expert, columnist, and author. Her most recent book is Clothes Sense: Straight Talk about Wardrobe Planning, *co-authored with Leslie Wood.*

Add a little sparkle to a favorite pullover or cardigan. Use pre-strung strands of sequins and metallic braid trim plus beaded appliqués, tiny nailhead studs, and fake faceted jewels to glamorize a sweater of wool jersey or soft sweater knit that you buy or make.

Team a long, full satin or taffeta skirt, supported by a lightweight crinoline petticoat, with a softly draped blouse in rabbit hair jersey.

Marriage of Fabric, Pattern & You

by Sandra Betzina

For a garment to be successful, four elements must enter into partnership: pattern, fabric, your figure, and your lifestyle. Because many home sewers do not like to shop, they may not be aware of what styles and fabrics are flattering to their figure. Making a garment without trying on a similar style in ready-to-wear is gambling with both time and money. Set aside two full days a year, one in spring and one in fall, to do nothing but try on clothes from ready-to-wear. Record in a notebook flattering and unflattering styles. Pay special attention to silhouettes, sleeve styling, seamlines, skirt and jacket lengths, as well as styling details that could be incorporated into your sewing. Addition of these details often makes the difference between an ordinary and extraordinary garment. Carry a 6" (15 cm) ruler, and use it to measure cuffs, collars, belts, plackets, pockets, or anything else you find that makes the style interesting.

Periodic breaks will give you an opportunity to absorb information and take notes for later reference. Do not attempt to go pattern and fabric shopping that day. You will be exhausted!

Observe fabric and style combinations and why they work. Designers pretest numerous fabrics before coming up with a salable item. Try to learn from their successes. If a style is flattering and the fabric is not, try to figure out what you don't like about the fabric and look for alternatives.

Amidst the ready-to-wear, look for fabrics that have a flattering drape, feel comfortable, and do not wrinkle. Pay attention to accessories. They give the final touch to the outfit and pull the whole look together.

When the pattern search begins, pattern purchases will no longer be impulsive. Study the line drawings on the pattern envelope. Look for style lines similar to those in ready-to-wear that you found flattering on you. If you are slightly overweight, any pattern with horizontal seamlines will make you look heavier. Look for vertical and asymmetrical style lines that can divide the silhouette and keep the eye moving up and down rather than across. If the pattern is described as "very loose fitting," consider buying it one size smaller to eliminate some of the style ease, scaling down the "big" look.

If you have broad shoulders or a large bust, a wide yoke will only draw attention to the problem. Raglan sleeves and boat necklines do not flatter narrow sloping shoulders. If your tummy is not flat, pleats and soft gathers will be kinder to your figure than tailored pants or a front yoke. Study the neckline and sleeve styling carefully. Would this pattern be more flattering on you with a neckline from another pattern? These things can be changed by overlaying one pattern on another. An unflattering or uncomfortable neckline may be the sole reason a garment hangs unworn in the closet.

If you have a tendency to make garments which when completed are simply "not me," here is a tip you might find useful. Cut your head from a photograph that can be superimposed over the model's head in the pattern book. Face it, these models are over 5' 8" (173 cm), weigh under 120 pounds (44.8 kg) and look good in anything. Once your own face is superimposed over the model's, you cannot be so easily fooled. Ask yourself these questions: Is this style really me? Where will I wear this? If you cannot think of enough occasions where you would feel comfortable in this garment, it is unlikely you will change your mind when the garment is completed.

If the pattern passes all these tests, it is a winner — compatible with your figure and lifestyle. Now, let's find the fabric. Before you begin a fabric search, you can eliminate many fabrics by careful analysis. Interesting styling and details show up better in a plain fabric. Prints are better showcased in simpler styling, interrupting the print with seams as little as possible.

Fabrics can be categorized as soft or crisp. A soft fabric drapes well and is kindest to the figure. Soft fabrics are mandatory for loose-fitting styles, gathers, soft pleats, wraps, and full skirts. Soft fabrics enable the garment to hang close to the body without broadening the silhouette. Soft fabric favorites are wool jersey, cotton interlock knits, rayon, wool crepe, wool and rayon challis, silk crepe de chine, silk broadcloth, silk noil, silk velvet, and tissue faille. Many sewers describe these as foolproof fabrics — fabrics that are always flattering on the body.

Crisp fabrics, on the other hand, are needed for structured styles to preserve the shape of the garment. A crisp fabric does not mold to the body but stands away and creates a silhouette on its own. Crisp fabrics are popular for coats, tailored jackets, straight skirts, and architectural shapes. Favorites are brocade, taffeta, worsted wool, and denim. Although some fabrics may feel soft, they actually fall under the crisp category because their drapability is limited. These fabrics include lightweight flannel, poplin, chino, chambray, and oxford cloth. Some fabrics are on the borderline between crisp and soft: damask, polyester/cottons, and other fabrics that may not be labeled.

Soft and Drapable Fabrics

Batiste	*Knits: interlock, jersey
*Broadcloth: cotton, silk, blends	*Silk-like polyester
*Challis: rayon, wool, blends	Silks: charmeuse, noil, velvet
*Crepe: polyester, wool	Tissue faille
*Crepe de chine	Velour

*Foolproof fabrics that are good in most styles

Crisp and Structured Fabrics

Brocade	Lawn
Chambray	Linen
Chino	Melton
Cotton sheeting	Mohair
Cotton shirting	Moire taffeta
Denim	Organdy
Double knits: cotton, wool, blends	Oxford cloth
	Poplin
Flannels: light & mediumweight	Silk tweed
	Sweatshirt fleece
Fleece	Taffeta
Gabardines: polyester, wool, blends	Wool: tweed, worsted, fleece
Lamé	Velvet: cotton, polyester

Your best bet in choosing the right fabric is a careful study of the pattern to determine whether a soft or crisp fabric is suitable. If you are having difficulty making a decision, check the fabric suggestions on the back of the pattern envelope. The first fabric mentioned is the fabric used in the designer original. You may not be able to find or want to use that exact fabric, but determining whether it is crisp or soft will aid in fabric selection. Check the chart for soft and crisp fabrics, and find a suitable substitute. Many interesting fabrics are hard to describe and label.

Analyze past garment failures. The culprit is often a fabric that is too stiff. When in doubt, choose a fabric that drapes and you will rarely be disappointed. One way to determine drapability is to drape the fabric over the shoulder across the bust. If no indication of the bust is in evidence, the fabric is crisp. If the fabric molds over the bust, the fabric is soft and has good drapability characteristics.

To confuse the fabric shopper even further is the issue of bottom and top weight. Some fabrics are simply too lightweight to be used for fitted skirts or pants. Two examples are batiste and lawn, which are simply too thin and lightweight to be successful. Outer weight fabrics such as mohair, melton, and fleece should be limited to garments such as coats and jackets. These fabrics are simply too bulky to be used for garments next to the body.

As you cruise around the fabric store, your choices are now limited by structure: soft and crisp. Pull out two or three bolts that interest you, and go over to the

mirror. Check for drapability first. With the fabric still draped over your shoulder, stand back several feet from the mirror. A fabric that seemed interesting at close range may be muddied from a distance. This effect often happens with tweeds and small prints. The very element you liked is lost in the distance translation.

Be careful of large prints and plaids. Will you be wearing the print, or will it be wearing you? Large prints are often more successful on the bottom, as in a full skirt, than on top close to the face. Unless you have strong coloring, a large, bold print may make you look washed out.

Is the fabric dressy or casual? Experienced sewers, who recognize fine fabrics, often make the mistake of choosing a fabric that is too dressy to suit their lifestyle and wardrobe needs. Be clear about the function of the garment in your wardrobe.

Now for the ultimate in willpower. Buy only ¼ yard (.25 m) of the fabric you are considering. Bring the fabric sample home. See how it fits with the accessories you already own. A $60 investment in fabric is nothing compared with the investment of shoes, belt, and purse if they are not already in your wardrobe. An interesting fabric in an odd color may drive you crazy trying to find accessories to match. It is often easier to match fabric to accessories than vice versa.

If you plan to make separates, take the fabric samples to your closet and see what works with what you currently own. Hang the fabric sample over your closet pole for a few days. Every time you get dressed, pretend you have already made the item in question. If you keep finding excuses about why the finished garment would be inappropriate,

Soft and Drapable

the fabric is probably too dressy, too bright, an uninspiring color, or incompatible with other clothes you own. Be glad that you bought only ¼ yard (.25 m) rather than the whole piece, and consider the exercise a good investment. On the other hand, if every time you open the closet you wish you had the completed garment, go to the store and purchase the fabric immediately.

Shopping can waste much time, so shop for fabric for outfits rather than separates. When buying fabric for a skirt, choose fabric for a blouse and jacket at the same time to eliminate separates that are wonderful but go with nothing you have in your wardrobe. Fabric cost, within reason, should not be a factor. The pleasure of working with and wearing a quality fabric is well worth the sacrifice. Make fewer items, perhaps, but buy the best fabric you can possibly afford.

Many sewers boast an extensive collection of fabrics that they keep stashed away in their "fabric aging room." Try to break yourself of this habit, which only stifles creativity and produces guilt. As long as you have a closet full of fabric, you will feel guilty about buying another piece of fabric. If you do succumb, you will feel you should use some of your old fabric first. The new fabric gets added to the collection, and the excitement is lost. Bag up any fabric you have had for over a year, and give it to charity. Moving fabric history out of your life will enable you to sew fabrics that are currently in fashion as well as enjoy the excitement of buying and sewing a piece of fabric in the same day.

Sandra Betzina writes a nationally syndicated sewing column and does a regular sewing segment on TV in San Francisco. She is the author of Power Sewing, New Ways to Make Fine Clothes Fast.

Crisp and Structured

Couture Sewing: The Perfect Touch

by Roberta Carr

Couture in its simplest form is the art of fine sewing. To the sewer it is a way to achieve perfection. The sewer who chooses couture knows that precision and accuracy are the stepping stones to success and can result in a beautiful garment to be worn with pride and admired by others.

Using couture methods is the ultimate expression of the sewer. Incorporated in the single word *couture* are design lines, fabric selection, construction to achieve permanence, and the art of shaping and pressing and using grain to fit. In custom sewing one must always consider the personality and body shape of the person who will wear the garment, the appropriateness of the design and fabric to the occasion, and the suitability to one's lifestyle. The combination of all these factors from selection, to construction, to the wearing of the garment is an exhilarating experience. What follows is a potpourri of couture techniques to support fine sewing.

Pants

Pants are easy to sew: all you need are four seams, a zipper, and a waistband. "Elementary, my dear Watson." However, the way these seams are sewn, pressed, and shaped makes the difference.

Pants seams should be sewn from hem to waist. The seams should be pressed flat on both sides to meld the thread before pressing open. Press the inseam open from hem to crotch, using a curved pressing tool for the last 6" to 8" (15 to 20.5 cm) near the crotch. A ham is good for this. Never clip the curve in the inseam. The slight pull prevents baggy pants in the back.

On a flat surface, press the side seam open from hem to hip. Then press from waist to hip over a ham. Clip the curve until the seam lies perfectly flat.

Roberta C. Carr, known as "Bobbie," is the owner of the Fabric Carr, a retail fabric store in Los Altos, California. Her writing has appeared in national sewing magazines.

How to Eliminate Baggy Knees

1) Identify the knee line with a basting stitch across the front pants leg. Pin the pants to an ironing board so the knee line is secure. Lay a damp press cloth on the pants from knee to hem, and steam. (This method is not suitable for fabrics that require matching.)

2) Hold the knee line in place, and pull on the hem to stretch the pants from knee to hem ⅜" (1 cm). This tightens the fibers and slightly narrows the leg. Dry completely before removing from board. Cut off the ⅜" (1 cm) so back and front pants leg will match.

Fine-tuning Pants

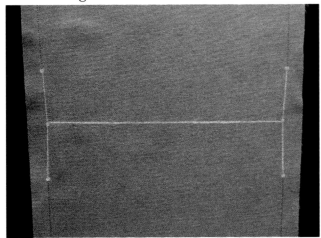

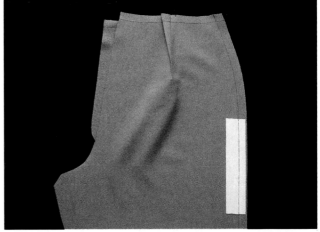

Create a pocket to reshape the pants leg and knee for perfect fit. Before sewing the side seam and inseam, mark the stitching line by making a dot 2" (5 cm) above and 2" (5 cm) below the knee line on the stitching line. At the knee line, mark in ⅛" (3 mm). Connect these points, using chalk and a French curve. Stitch, following the new chalk line. Press seam open; you may need to clip seam allowance to make seam lie flat. From the side, the pants leg will appear straight.

Cut a bias piece of tightly woven sew-in interfacing 1½" (3.8 cm) wide and approximately 7" (18 cm) long. Strip will fill in hollow just below the hip on the side of the leg. Not noticeable in skirts, the hollow almost always shows in pants. Pin interfacing on the wrong side of the back of the pants so ½" (1.3 cm) falls in the seam allowance and 1" (2.5 cm) is on the garment. This bias piece will automatically be sewn into the seam permanently and will hold out the side seam for a smooth silhouette.

Gathering Ruffles

Fashion 1988 screams ruffles: small narrow ruffles, wide full ruffles. Whatever the size or length to be gathered, it is always best to gather in sections. This makes gathering easier, and also if the thread breaks, you then need to regather only a small section.

One of the problems in gathering in sections is preventing a blank space from appearing where the sections meet. This blank space can be eliminated by gathering so the sections overlap. This technique can be done whether you use two rows or three rows of gathering. The secret for perfectly even gathers is always to be sure the gathering stitches of the two rows are exactly parallel to each other. Start and stop each row in the same place.

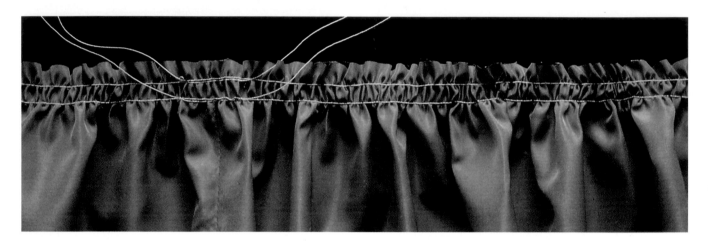

Darts

The close-to-the-body look can be achieved with darts, a major way to shape garments. Sewing a dart correctly ensures a smooth look without a pucker at the end. The traditional two-thread method is to stitch from the wide end to the point. Avoid any backstitching, which may produce a pucker. A long thread tail eliminates knot tying and prevents the stitches from pulling out. Sheer fabrics require single-thread stitching, which prevents unsightly thread tail show-through. This is also an excellent technique for any darts or tucks stitched on the right side of a garment, a stylish detail that gives a fashion look to simple garments.

Two-thread Darts

Stitch from wide end for ½" (1.3 cm) at 20 stitches per inch (2.5 cm). Change to stitch length for fabric, and continue to within ½" (1.3 cm) of point. Shorten stitches, and stitch close to fold. Continue stitching off fabric for 3" (7.5 cm). Cut thread, leaving tail.

Single-thread Darts

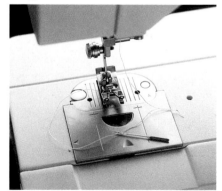

1) Thread machine except for the needle. Remove needle, and thread from back side with bobbin thread; replace needle. Tie bobbin thread to top thread; wind 10" to 15" (25.5 to 38 cm) of bobbin thread onto spool. Bobbin thread and top thread are now one.

2) Sew dart from point, making sure first stitch is exactly on folded edge of the dart point. Shorten stitch length for first ½" (1.3 cm). Repeat threading procedure for each dart. (Contrasting thread is used to show detail.)

Princess Seams

An increasing number of princess designs are appearing in all pattern company collections. It's an ideal way to get a close-to-the-body look with a style that is flattering on all body types. A princess seam is the conversion of a dart into a seamline. The result is a curved seam that must be sewn to another curved seam. It is not an easy task to achieve a smooth, attractive seam when you are working from the inside of a garment.

How to Shape a Princess Seam

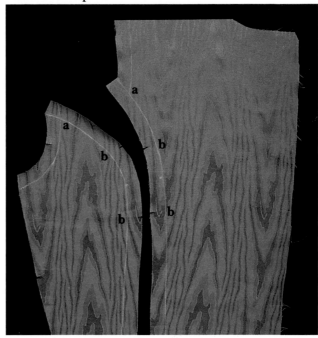

1) Mark the stitching line on both pieces of the princess garment on the *right* side of the fabric. It is also critical to mark all match points: **(a)** seam intersections, **(b)** notches and dots.

2) Fold under seam allowance on curved edge. Place straighter piece on ham, right side up. Clip curve on straighter piece, if necessary. Match folded edge to stitching line; pin at right angle to stitching line. Slip-stitch seam; stitching will show on wrong side, allowing you to machine-stitch accurately.

Wide Scalloped Seam for Support

The couturiers in Paris frequently use a wide scalloped seam on lightweight fabrics such as wool crepe or sheer wool to give solid support to side seams. It gives a sleek look to the finished garment.

Cut side seams with 1" to 1¼" (2.5 to 3.2 cm) seam allowances. Stitch, and press the seam open. With pinking shears, trim the seam allowance in a series of scallops about 2½" (6.5 cm) long, curving in to within ¼" (6 mm) of the stitching line and out to 1" (2.5 cm) at the fullest part of the scallop. The scallop serves the purpose of clipping, allows the seam to lie flat even if it is curved, but does not diminish the strength and support of the seam.

Scalloped seam adds a couture touch.

Skirts

With the advent of more structured designs and the rebirth of the suit, skirts become increasingly important. A perfect fitting skirt is a basic garment in a well-thought-out wardrobe. Comfort is most important in making a skirt wearable, and it starts with the waistband. Looks are important, too. Interfacing the hem of a straight or slightly flared skirt gives body, weight, and a finished look without hem stitches showing through to the right side of the garment. Choose a woven sew-in interfacing for medium to heavyweight fabrics; choose organza for light to mediumweight fabrics.

How to Shape a Waistband

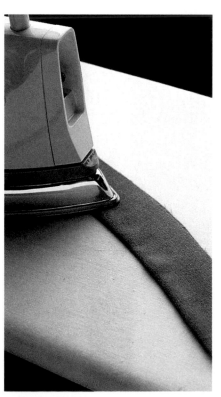

1) Cut waistband on the crosswise grain. Fold in half lengthwise; press foldline lightly. Using a damp press cloth, apply steam to fabric.

2) Use pressure from iron, and pull on waistband to curve folded edge so it becomes smaller than raw edge. Continue across waistband, overlapping sections. Set shape with dry iron; let dry completely.

3) Cut interfacing on bias. For fusible, follow manufacturer's instructions to apply; reshape waistband. For sew-in, shape interfacing to match waistband curve, and apply.

How to Interface a Hem

1) Cut bias strips the width of hem allowance plus 1¼" (3.2 cm). Mark hemline. Lay strips on garment so ⅝" (1.5 cm) falls in hem allowance and remainder is on skirt. Pin interfacing to skirt on hemline.

2) Fold back the ⅝" (1.5 cm) of interfacing that is in the hem allowance; slipstitch to hemline. Pin top of interfacing to skirt ⅝" (1.5 cm) below cut edge. Turn back and slipstitch interfacing to skirt.

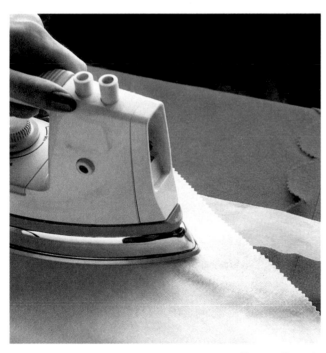

3) Turn up hem; press lightly. For an A-line or flared skirt, you may need to shrink hem allowance. Slip a piece of brown paper under hem allowance; using a damp press cloth, press lightly to shrink hem.

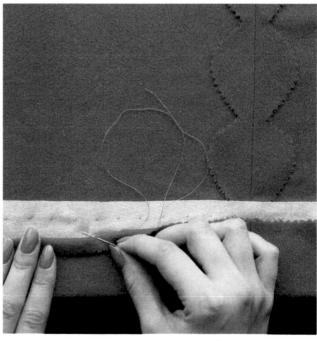

4) Finish hem edge by pinking, serging, or using hem tape. Slipstitch hem to interfacing. The interfacing will show ⅝" (1.5 cm) above finished hem edge. This provides a grade and prevents hem from showing through to right side.

Accessories: The Final Touch

by Donna Salyers

Accessories are an integral part of dressing; with that final touch, the outfit makes perfect sense. Even the most expensive garment will improve with the addition of accessories.

The cost of ready-made accessories can quickly wreak havoc with any wardrobe budget. Yet the cost of materials to make accessories is minimal, and you need not be an expert sewer. Patience, as well as persistence, is a virtue when it comes to finding just the right color and fabric for making accessories. However, you would probably spend an equal amount of time hunting through ready-to-wear accessories for just the right look.

Handbags

An elegant Ultrasuede® handbag that sells in a boutique for $100 can be created for far, far less. The bag shown, with finished dimensions of 13" by 8½" (33 by 21.8 cm), is only a beginning. Have fun piecing together Ultrasuede scraps, stitching a monogram, or combining Ultrasuede with snakeskin.

Supplies
12" (30.5 cm) metal snap-close frame.
¼ yard (.25 m) Ultrasuede.
¼ yard (.25 m) each of lining, fleece, fusible web, and stiff interfacing.
Glue stick, thread.

✄ Cutting Directions

Cut two rectangles each of Ultrasuede, fleece, and fusible web 13½" × 9" (34.3 × 23 cm) for bag. Cut two lining strips of Ultrasuede 13½" × 2" (34.3 × 5 cm). Cut two rectangles each of lining and interfacing 13½" × 7½" (34.3 × 19.3 cm). Cut two casing strips of Ultrasuede 11" × 1" (28 × 2.5 cm).

How to Make a Handbag

1) Fuse fleece to wrong side of bag pieces by sandwiching fusible web between fleece and bag. Fuse interfacing to wrong side of lining.

2) Center casing strips on lining strips, and secure with glue stick. Topstitch each long edge. Stitch a lining strip to each bag piece, wrong sides together, with ¼" (6 mm) seam. Stitch long edges of lining pieces to each free edge of lining strip.

3) Align the two rectangles, right sides together, matching seams. Stitch, leaving a 5" (12.5 cm) centered opening at base of lining. Turn right side out.

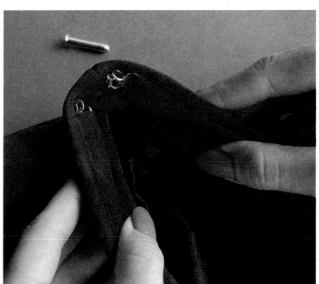

4) Fold lining seam allowances to inside; match edges, and topstitch. Smooth lining to inside. Remove metal pins from ends of frame, and insert frame in casing. Replace pins.

Belts

Copy ready-to-wear with Ultrasuede®, which can be purchased by the inch, making it very economical. Two or three inches of 45" (115 cm) Ultrasuede is adequate for waist sizes up to 40" (102 cm), depending on the style of belt.

For a sash, cut a strip of Ultrasuede (traditional weight or Facile®) 15" (38 cm) longer than the waist measurement, and about 2" (5 cm) wide. Trim the ends to desired shape. Using a serger, finish the edges with matching or contrasting thread. Tighten the lower looper tension so the thread rolls around to the wrong side. Use liquid fray preventer on threads, allow to dry, and trim.

Reptile skin scraps and a buckle blank transform Ultrasuede into a luxurious belt. Cut an Ultrasuede strip 3" (7.5 cm) wide and 3" (7.5 cm) longer than the waist measurement. Press ⅜" (1 cm) on the long edges to the wrong side; baste with glue stick, and topstitch. Trace the buckle on the back of the reptile skin, taking care that the scales are attractively positioned. Add a ⅜" (1 cm) margin. Apply rubber cement to the wrong side of the skin and the face of the buckle. Once the cement is tacky, place the buckle on the traced outline. Apply cement to the edges of the buckle back; smooth the skin to the buckle back,

clipping as necessary. Finish the buckle back with Ultrasuede cut to fit the buckle. Make slits for the buckle hooks, and glue in place. Thread the ends through buckle rings; adjust to fit, and secure with stitching. Trim excess.

Scarves

A lace scarf moves easily from cashmere sweater sets to flannel shirts. A beginning sewer can quickly make this a first project, because lace doesn't ravel and it hides a multitude of stitching sins.

Supplies
1⅜ yards (1.30 m) point d'esprit or lace.
3 yards (2.75 m) lace trim, 1" (2.5 cm) wide.

Sources:
Handbag frames, patterns, accessories, and notions: *Ghee's*, Suite 205, 106 E. Kings Highway, Shreveport, LA 71104. Buckle blanks, reptile and leather scraps by the pound: *Quintessence*, Box 723554, Atlanta, GA 30339; catalog, $2.

Donna Salyers is a TV personality, author, and lecturer. Her twice-weekly newspaper column is syndicated by The Chicago Tribune.

How to Make a Scarf

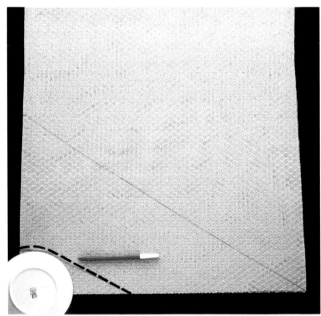

1) Fold fabric in half crosswise. Cut 15" by 24" (38 by 61 cm) triangle for scarf. Cut 4" by 9" (10 by 23 cm) triangle from lower edge, with cut edge slightly curved so scarf will lie smooth at neck.

2) Lap and pin trim over scarf ½" (1.3 cm), clipping around motifs as necessary for trim to lie smooth on curves and angles. Machine-stitch with narrow zigzag or short straight stitch ¼" (6 mm) inside edges. On wrong side, trim scarf close to stitching. Repair clips with machine stitching.

Silk scarf. From the lightest, softest fabric available, cut a 36" (91.5 cm) square. Although edges might be finished with a hand or serged rolled hem, a ¼" (6 mm) fringe is more desirable because it doesn't add weight. Once scarf is cut to its finished shape, simply pull threads to create fringe.

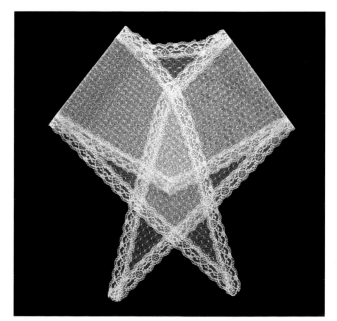

Lace Scarf. Choose point d'esprit or an all-over lace for a lace-on-lace scarf to tie at the neck for a look of English elegance.

Wool muffler. Make a soft wool muffler for everyone on your gift list. You can make four mufflers with 1¼ yards (1.15 m) of fine, 60" (150 cm) wool. Straighten ends by pulling a cross thread and trimming evenly along pulled threads. Draw cutting lines on fabric, 15" (38 cm) apart, parallel with selvages. Cut four strips, each 15" by 45" (38 by 115 cm). Zigzag with a short and narrow stitch close to each long edge and across each short end at top of desired fringe depth. Fringe short ends by pulling away cross threads up to stitching.

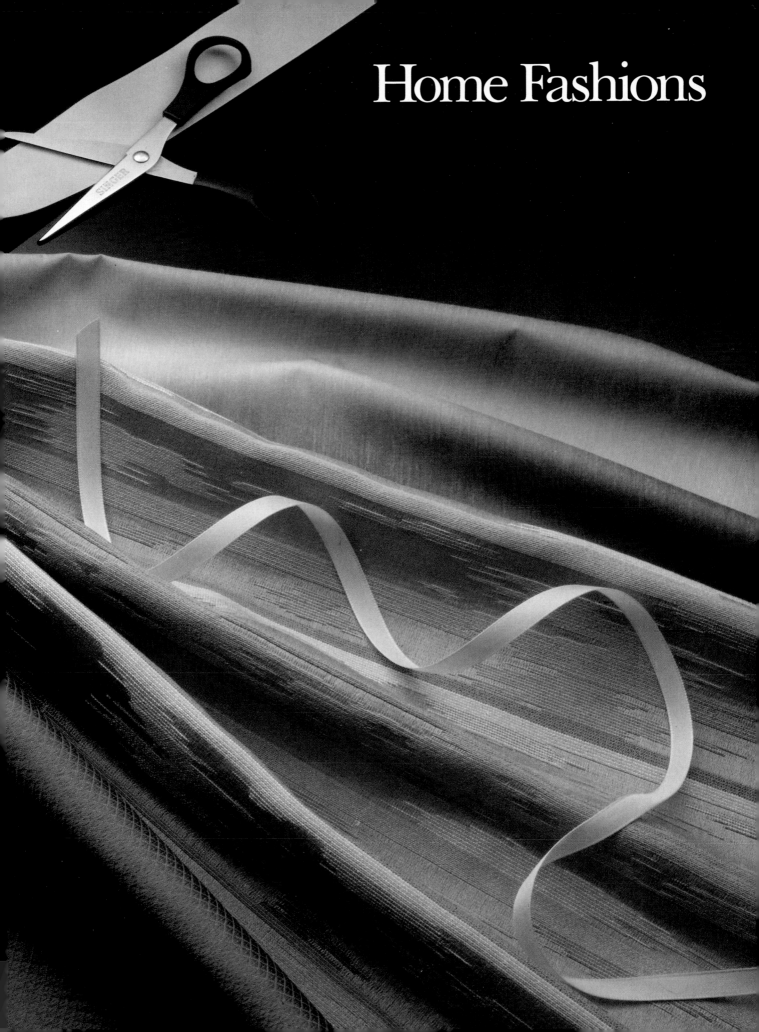

Home Fashions

Home Fashion Trends

by Pati Simon Gelfman

More than ever, with the frenzied pace of the world beyond our front doors, homes today have taken on a critical role. Those in the work force, including 49 million working women, look to the homestead for comfort. It's the place to snuggle on the sofa in a good-natured room that soothes weary nerves.

It's no surprise, then, that modern styles are reminiscent of simpler times and places. New rooms are designed to look faded and mellow. Comfy and worn, informal yet gracious. Today, updating a decorating scheme means back-dating to romance or returning to the refuge of the country.

Anything goes in home fashions, as long as the surroundings are sink-in comfortable. From the European countryside to the American West, the look is playful and eclectic. Grandma's turn-of-the-century sofa works beautifully with a leopard print footstool in an artful mix of unmatched furnishings.

English and French country styles with their yards of ruffled floral chintz continue as popular home fashions. "I think, however, that we're becoming very proud of anything American, particularly folk art," says Priscilla Miller, vice president of the Home Sewing Division of Concord Fabrics. Miller sees a new version of country Americana emerging that emphasizes cross-stitch simplicity with sun-baked textiles, Sante Fe style, giving a new definition to the designs of the American West.

Old World opulence, like the drawing room of a Victorian English castle, is a fresh influence in home fashion. Swags, cornices, and tiebacks are lavishly trimmed to the nines in fringes and tassels. Long draperies are back in frosted fabrics such as chintz and moire, which fall into a luxurious puddle on the floor.

Wherever you look in the home, fabric captures the eye. Balloon shades and billowy window coverings often replace hard window treatments, such as blinds and louvered shutters. Roman shades take on a soft, new look, topped with flowing swags and jabots. Slipcovers are back. Pillows fall into a luscious tumble on the bed. Quilts are decorated with delicate appliqué.

Lightweight cotton chintz is everywhere, but elegant fabrics such as brocades, silks, tapestry, and velvets are enjoying a revival. Fussy lace panels are threaded across windows or sewn onto pillows. Even technology plays a hand in creating luminescent fabrics with a light, pearlized look.

What's new in fabric prints? There's no end in sight to the popularity of the bold botanicals such as the cabbage roses of French florals, mixed and matched with tiny prints of paisleys, plaids, and stripes.

Nature is fashionable again in textiles. Winning motion pictures have lured once-tame decorating tastes into the jungles of Africa and the Australian Outback. Exotic fabric prints feature leopard skins, elephants, and zebras.

Animals are everywhere. Ducks, deer, and sport fish motifs play into the expected return to the masculine den. In the future, look for a popularized return of shells and nauticals.

Along with bold prints, trims are an easy and important way to add fine detailing to home furnishings, says Bill Lanahan, president of Europa Imports, a company that markets trims from England, Switzerland, and Germany. The historical use of home fashion trims is in placemats and bedding.

Today, however, ruffles, fringes, tassels, eyelet, embroidered ribbons, jacquard woven braids, and lace decorate everything from curtains to lampshades. Metallic braids and cording, popular in Europe, are beginning to show up in the United States in such unexpected places as borders on draperies and pillows. Trims are available in soft pastels that complement the color trends of home decorating.

Old World Opulence

Photograph courtesy of Waverly Fabrics

The Color Palette of Home Fashions

Like the length of hemlines, home fashion colors change over the years. Thankfully, these color changes are less frequent than those of the apparel industry. Trends in home fashion color are reasonably predictable. Preferences seem to work sequentially around the color wheel. The shifting color wheel tends to repeat itself every twenty to thirty years. For example, turquoise and black, which debuted with art deco in the twenties, reappeared in the fifties and returned in the eighties.

After a decade of colorless, neutral decorating, there is a new-found confidence to use color in the home in an individualized way. "Colors are put together today that you would never have imagined," says Connie Meyer, manager of the Hirshfield-Warner designer showroom in Minneapolis. There are unexpected harmonies in floral prints that combine pink, purple, green, and a splash of orange, all in the right intensities. Gone are the days when a duo of colors, such as avocado and gold or pink and gray, dominated home fashions from cafe curtains to bathroom tile.

The color wheel is shifting to the warmer side. Pastels in warm and cool versions are as romantic as ever in peach, lavender, pale yellow, and misty green. Blues, tinted in the medium ranges, have fresh names such as country French, Williamsburg, or dusty blue. Ruby, amethyst, emerald, sapphire, and gold bring a medley of jewelry-box colors into the home as do metallic threads woven through fabrics.

Where will the color wheel turn next? "It's a favorite term to write that a certain color will be 'in' this year, when actually it is only an influencing pigment that is changing the other colors on the palette," says Darlene Kinning, a color stylist for Colwell/General Inc., a major manufacturer of color charts for paint and window coverings. Kinning is a respected color forecaster who is a member of the Color Marketing Group and the International Colour Authority. Both organizations have a national and international influence on color trends, from home fashions to the automotive industry.

In the years ahead, she predicts that red will continue to be strong in its various sun-drenched southwestern colors, such as peach, coral, and clay. Old English pinks and plums will prevail in popularity as will clear pinks and soft lavenders. Cranberry will see a revival.

Color charts are used to select and match colors.

Photograph courtesy of Waverly Fabrics

Mauve, while still around, will soften into peachy beige. Yellows will be understated and primarily seen in soft, creamy tones. Bright yellows and oranges will be used in low doses as accent colors.

Greens will enter center stage in sage brush, yellow-green, khaki, and deep jade. Blue-greens, à la art deco, range from light to dark but a headline color will be a flattering teal. Expect to see a collection of blues from grayed tones to sapphire.

Neon brights will mellow into more palatable shades, while earthtones such as desert green, yellowed tan, and khaki will radiate color. A yellowed version of taupe is expected to become the new neutral, while updated tones of gray will remain popular.

Why all this fuss about home fashion color? Color has a subliminal and psychological effect. Blue, the anchor hue of home decorating, is generally accepted as a calming color. Fall colors, including red in its clay tones, are down-to-earth and reassuring. The bright colors of spring have high vitality and are used in functional rooms, such as the kitchen and bath. The undemanding colors of summer, such as peach, rosy pink, and pale yellow, are perfect for bedrooms.

Countless wardrobes have been influenced by the popular notion of personal color analysis — a system that identifies an individual's skin tone and links it to one of the color schemes of summer, fall, winter, and spring. This same process is finding its way into the interior decoration of the home to produce a color scheme that is in harmony with the personalities of the inhabitants.

Photograph courtesy of Waverly Fabrics

English/French Country Style

Updating with Color, Fabric & Trim

Part of the joy of decorating is its infinite possibilities. But along with those possibilities are some genuine challenges: How can you give a lift to an existing decor with these new colors and fabrics?

Many professional designers believe that the easiest way to establish a color scheme is to select an upholstery or drapery fabric that has an attractive blend of colors. It's easy, then, to match paint, wallcoverings, carpet colors, and accessories.

To update a sagging decor, use trims to bring in new colors and textures. One effective way to do this is to apply a wide ribbon braid as if it were wallpaper border to the wall of, for example, the dining room. Repeat the same trim in other areas of the room — in placemats, tablecloths, or cushions.

In other areas of the house, embroidered ribbons or soft lace can be glued to the slats of stark mini-blinds for a feminine look. To soften the lines of wooden shutters, blinds, and shades, consider adding dainty side draperies or a swag and jabots of floral chintz or stately paisley. Ribbon roses can be mounted to Roman shades or drapery cornices.

Why not stitch an artful collection of buttons on quilts, pillows, or window treatments? To revitalize lifeless draperies, cafe curtains, or shades, add a border of French ribbons, intricate braid, ruffles, lace, or fringe. Vertical rows of eyelet hand-stitched to a Roman shade turn bland to romantic. Add trims such as tassels and fringe to sofa cushions and lampshades as a throwback to a more serene era.

Accent pillows, trimmed with ruffles, braids, lace, or appliqué, are an easy way to bring new vitality to a room, and quilts capture the country look.

Slipcovers in a fresh new fabric may be a perfect way to restore life to tired furniture. Reserve the effort, however, for substantial pieces in good condition. Choose durable, mediumweight fabrics such as chintz, gabardine, ticking, toiles, linen, or damask. Another advantage of slipcovers? They allow a quick change from stiff cushions and pillows to more comfortable types that are down or polyester-filled.

To take the guesswork out of home decorating, many companies offer a collection of coordinated fabrics for home sewers. They have extensive collections of large floral fabrics that mix and match beautifully with tiny patterns, stripes, checks, and paisleys.

Patti Simon Gelfman is a Minneapolis based teacher and freelance writer. Her work appears in The Family Handyman *and several business publications.*

Curtain Calls: New Ideas for Your Windows

by Susan Meyers

Soft is the word for this year's new look in window treatments; fabric is used to add grace and charm to plain-jane windows that have begun to look neglected and boring. Sumptuous fabrics are shirred, folded, wrapped, pouffed, draped, tucked, or puddled into elegant window fashions that do their part to make a room look beautiful. Although pleated draperies remain a standard, variety is now the key to a custom look that adds just the right degree of softness to a room. The softness may come from a curtain, drapery, or fabric shade used alone; or it may derive from the creative layering of one or more of these with a valance or a swag and jabots. Whatever the combination, the result is a fresh new focus on detail: the heading, the hang, the length, the trim.

Major emphasis is on the heading of the window treatment, with shirred and draped headings being two of the most widely used, but new lengths have caught the eye, too. Today, floor-length is no longer synonymous with full-length. Whenever romantic, billowing curtains would look skimpy at traditional floor-length, make them at least 12" to 24" (30.5 to 61 cm) longer to spill onto the floor like a bridal veil.

The good news for the home sewer is that these soft window dressings, which may look as if they required the wand of a magician to achieve, are easier to sew than traditional pinch pleated draperies, and some of the newer treatments are virtually no-sew projects. Curtains that are shirred or wrapped on a rod require less precise fitting than tailored draperies, and the puddled lengths require less precise measuring. These styles are also more adaptable to different window sizes, an advantage for those who move often but want to personalize the decor of their windows with each move. From voluminous romantic sheers to precisely tailored shades, the variations in style suit every nuance of personal taste and every level of sewing experience.

Softly Romantic

The biggest trend in this year's soft window treatments is the romantic look, with its graceful cascades or generous poufs of fabric. Part of the appeal is that the romantic window enhances many decorating schemes. Not only does it soften a contemporary decor, but it dresses up the country look and adds the finishing touch to French country, English country, and Victorian interiors, just to name a few.

Swags and jabots. "Swags are back in a variety of styles," says Lynn Marquardt, owner of Made to Order, custom sewing for decorators. "Some are the traditional, formal treatment; but a lot of them are very informal." To create informal elegance, use a single swag panel, lined in self-fabric or contrasting fabric, and loop it loosely two or more times over a rod — and even casually tie it in a large knot or two for show; use a decorative rod, wooden pole, or plain rod covered with matching shirred fabric. For a more formal look, use jabots alongside a centered swag, draped in neat, balanced folds. A layered treatment of swags, jabots, and draperies is a rich, formal look that may appear complicated to put together, but simply involves hanging the rod for the draperies beneath a mounting board used for the swag and jabots.

Softly Romantic

Photograph courtesy of Waverly Fabrics

Specialty windows. Not all windows are single rectangular units. Those that aren't — bow, bay, and arched (or Palladian) windows, for example — call for creative modifications of curtains and draperies. A romantic window covering often works well because of its adaptability. Filmy sheer curtains are perfect for bow windows, because they help define the bow shape instead of hiding it. The only special hardware needed is a rod that bends to fit the curved window. For bay windows,

swags can do the job of tying the windows together into one unit. Jabots can fall either along the two outer edges of the bay or between each window to emphasize the shape of the bay. If you use curtains along with the swag and jabot, they can be hung on a rod specially angled for bay windows.

Sheer curtains hanging from the arch of a Palladian window emphasize the curve of the window; the sheer

Palladian Window with Sunburst Effect

Shirred or pouffed valances, shades, and curtains. "If the home sewer is looking for a technique to be successful with, the deep shirred heading is one of the best to give a classy look," says professional drapery installer Paul TenEyck of Aero Draperies. TenEyck credits the popularity of this heading with the availability of the deep, flat Continental® rod. Where one Continental rod gives depth to a heading, two Continental rods double the depth. The double Continental valance is popular at Calico Corners®, nationwide retail stores for home furnishing fabrics. This heading consists of two adjoining rod pockets separated only by a seam across the middle of the valance; the rods are hung ½" (1.3 cm) apart.

TenEyck hangs many traditional two-rod valances, which can be styled flat or pouffed depending on the length of the valance and the look preferred. You can also achieve endless combinations by stacking rods of differing widths; fabric-covered rods can be stacked with decorative rods, such as the Cirmosa®, for a custom valance.

Cloud and balloon valances are widely used for a full, romantic look. Which is which? you may ask, because the two terms are often confused. A cloud valance is shirred at the top and pouffed at the bottom, creating a loose, billowy effect, whereas the balloon valance has inverted pleats that fall into relaxed folds. Even more widely used are the cloud and balloon shades, which provide the style of a romantic window and the practicality of light control all in one.

Besides valances, the shirred heading is versatile for curtains such as bishop sleeves. The rounded poufs of this curtain are shaped from a straight panel of fabric. Create the flounces by tying the fabric with cord or slipping it through large wooden curtain rings; then drape the fabric over the cord or rings. Bishop sleeve curtains are especially attractive with a flared bottom puddled gracefully onto the floor. Use a string to get a quick length measurement, as suggested by Lynn Marquardt: "Drape the string the way you want the curtain to look, and then measure the string. This method works for all sorts of curtains."

Lace. Nothing is more romantic than lace. White or ecru lace panels, and even lace or lace-trimmed tablecloths, can lend a European flair to a window. To show off the beauty of the fabric, use see-through rods and measure the fabric one and one-half times the fullness, or twice the fullness for sheers with a lace lower edge. Laces are available in widths up to 118" (295 cm) for a seamless curtain. Dutch and other no-sew laces, which come in lengths from 9" to 84" (23 to 210 cm) have prefinished rings or holes to slip the rod through. Simply use liquid fray preventer on the cut edges. Laces also readily complement and trim other fabrics when used as cafe sashes, ruffles, or bows.

can be hung from a special bent rod and loosely tied back to one or both sides. For a sunburst effect, tie a short sheer in a knot at the bottom of the arch, and use a cafe curtain over the lower one-third of the window. Another choice is to hang a curtain from a straight rod just below the arch, leaving the arch uncovered; this is a simple way to gain privacy without covering the whole window.

Tailored Softness

Maybe you want to update your window treatments, but the romantic look is not for you. "You can still use fabric as a top treatment over simple shades and blinds," says Lynn Marquardt. She explains that the fabric, the trim, and the way the treatment is hung can make the difference between romantic opulence and tailored elegance. For traditional decor, swags and jabots can be plainly draped. Or pull a simple scarf swag through jumbo rings at the upper corners of the window. This short swag is especially attractive when it is repeated on several windows. Use it alone or over blinds, shades, or pleated draperies as a quick way to soften the overall look of the room. For a contemporary decor, a simple valance makes an ideal top treatment.

Tailored draperies can often be updated with trims and details, such as tiebacks. For a complete change, you may decide to replace the draperies entirely with Roman shades or stationary curtains. "The hobbled Roman shade is nice, as it allows someone with a contemporary room to add a little softness," explains Pat Forsha of Calico Corners®. "And the half-stitched Roman shade gives a neat, precise look, because the stitching provides an automatic pleat line."

Tab top, tie top, and tent-flap panels are other tailored window coverings that highlight the style of either traditional or contemporary decor. Besides being practical, the goal for these easy-to-sew treatments is to dress the window with style, yet maintain the integrity of uncluttered simplicity.

Tailored Softness

Photograph courtesy of Calico Corners®

Stuff poufs and flounces with polyester fiberfill for extra body.

Dressing Up Your Windows

Professional drapery makers and stylists call it "dressing down" — hand-adjusting and training a window treatment so it will hang beautifully, just like the ones in the decorating magazines. With so many styles available to the home sewer, Paul TenEyck emphasizes that "half the know-how is choosing the right hardware and getting it all hung right." The following are some tips for sewing, mounting, and dressing down your window treatments to dress up your windows:

- Line curtains, swags, cascades, and valances to add body and improve the way they hang.

- Use weights or weighted tapes in hems of full-length curtains to make them hang straight down or to give the lower edge a flared shape.

- Staple swags and cascades in place on a mounting board to hold folds in place.

- To mimic the look of a swag, make an easy-to-sew shaped valance that drops in a curve at the center and tapers to a longer length at the sides.

- For a seamless valance, use a fabric that can be railroaded (so the selvages run at both the top and bottom).

- Train Roman, balloon, and cloud shades by raising them, hand-adjusting the folds and poufs, and leaving the shades raised for several days or up to two weeks.

- Add banding, stenciling, or a valance to dress up a flat Roman shade. A bias tape maker can be used to make the banding; instead of folding the fabric in half as for tape, just use the flat band of fabric with the edges turned in.

- Keep full or heavy tieback curtains looking fresh, and not pinched or crushed against the wall, by using either tieback hooks (which are longer than cup hooks) or tieback supports, which can be adjusted in depth.

Susan Meyers is a freelance editor and writer based in Minneapolis; she is an editor for the Singer Sewing Reference Library.

Sew a Comforter Cover from Sheets

by Kathy Davis Ellingson

A comforter, duvet, or hyggelig cover is a removable sheet or fabric casing that protects your comforter and gives you the option of changing the look of a bedroom as quickly as changing your sheets. In less than an hour, with two flat sheets, you can make an envelope-style cover to custom-fit your comforter. Bedmaking is simplified since a top sheet is no longer needed.

Select a sheet with a decorative border, and use the border to your advantage. It eliminates stitching on one end and quickly provides a custom trim.

Before cutting, consider sheet design if matching stripes, plaids, or other designs. The finished cover size is 2" (5 cm) narrower and 2" (5 cm) shorter than the comforter to give a snug, puffy fit. Use another top sheet to make coordinating shams for your pillows.

Kathy Davis Ellingson operates Davis Design, a five-year-old business that produces custom-sewn home furnishings for individual clients and store accounts in Minneapolis.

Supplies				
Comforter Size	**Sheets**	**Hook and Loop Tape**	**Plastic Rings**	**Ribbons**
Twin	2 twin flats	7" (18 cm)	6	3 yards (2.75 m)
Full	2 full flats	9" (23 cm)	6	3 yards (2.75 m)
Queen	2 queen flats	11" (28 cm)	10	5 yards (4.60 m)
King	2 king flats	13" (33 cm)	10	5 yards (4.60 m)

How to Sew a Comforter Cover

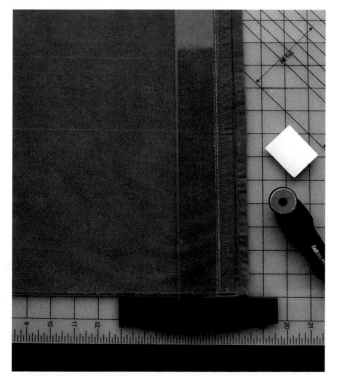

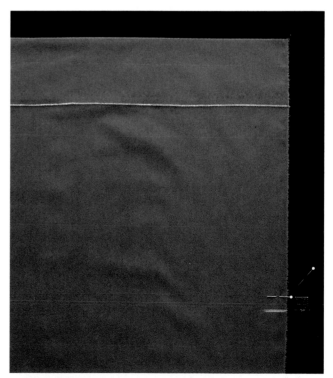

1) Cut both sheets 1" (2.5 cm) wider than finished cover width. With bordered edges even, fold one sheet in half lengthwise, aligning side edges along a straight edge. Square, mark, and trim lower edge.

2) Measure from squared lower edge to finished cover length; add ¾" (2 cm), and mark with pin on both sides.

(Continued on next page)

How to Sew a Comforter Cover (continued)

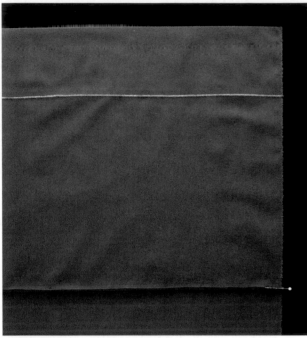

3) Fold sheet crosswise at pins, right sides together, and press. Stitch ¼" (6 mm) from fold. Fold again at stitching line, *wrong* sides together. This is the flap and back of cover.

4) Square, mark, and trim second sheet. For designed sheet, square end that continues flap design. Press under ½" (1.3 cm) twice, and stitch. This is the front of the cover.

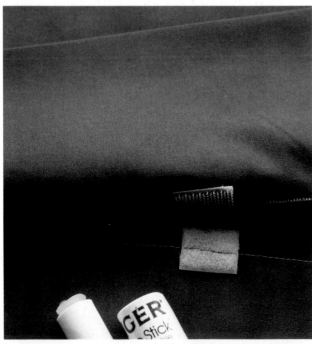

7) Glue 1" (2.5 cm) piece of hook side of tape to stitching line at marks on wrong side of flap. Glue 1" (2.5 cm) piece of loop half of tape to right side of front on hem edge at marks. Stitch through center of each tape; backstitch at each end.

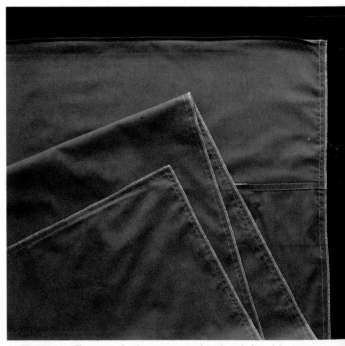

8) Reverse flap, and pin to cover back, right sides together. Pin cover front to back, right sides together, lining up lower edges. Stitch ½" (1.3 cm) from raw edges around three sides of cover; finish raw edges.

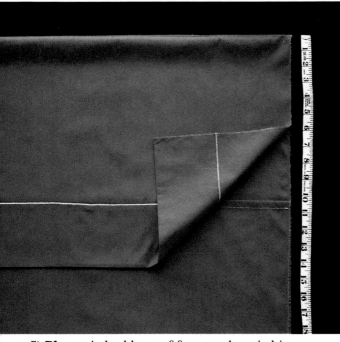

5) Place stitched hem of front under stitching on flap, and pin. Measure from upper edge to finished cover length, and add ½" (1.3 cm). Square, mark, and trim lower edge.

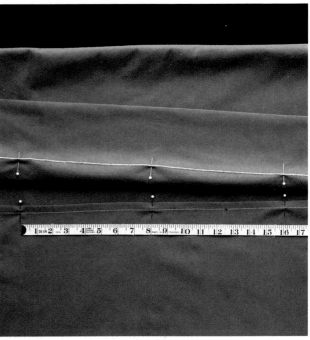

6) Mark placement for hook and loop tape on hem of front and stitching line of flap. Starting at the center, mark every 8" (20.5 cm).

9) Stitch rings to corners and center of upper and lower edges of comforter. For queen or king size, use two more rings, evenly spaced.

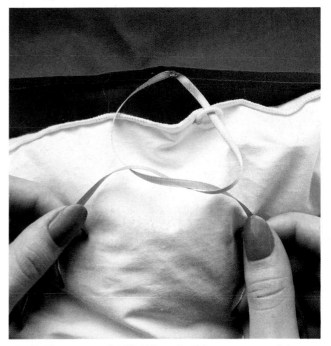

10) Tack center of 18" (46 cm) ribbons to matching areas on seam allowances of cover. Turn right side out. Insert comforter. Tie ribbons through rings to prevent shifting of comforter.

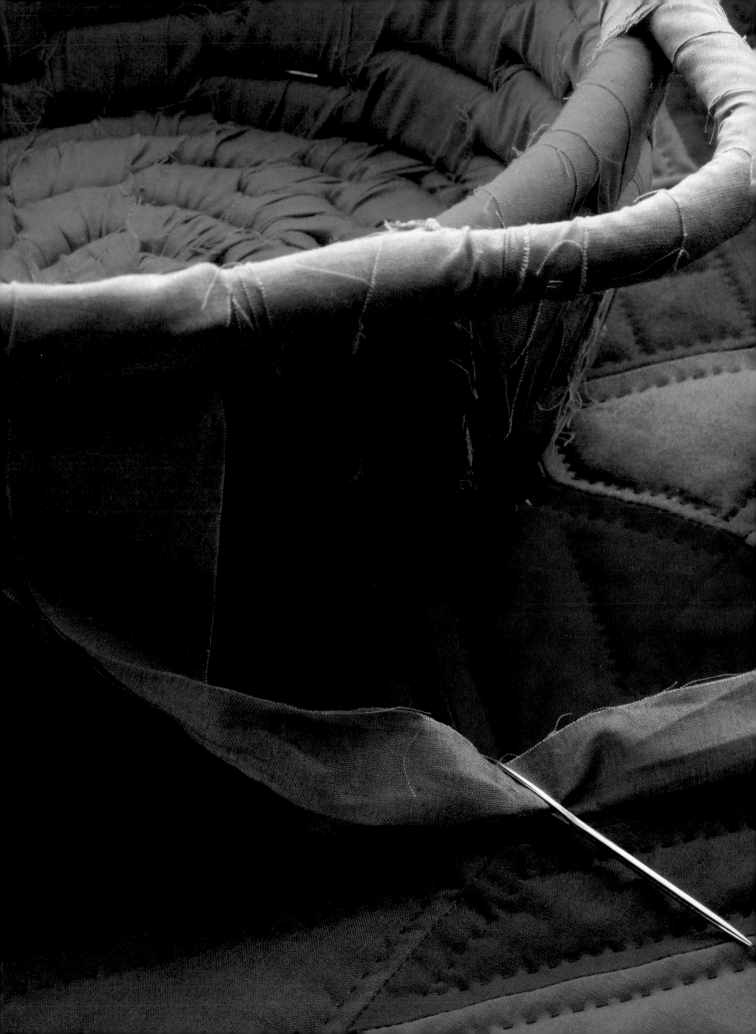

Fiber Art

Express Yourself with Fiber

by Dorothy Martin

Crafting may be the one thing we do for our own personal enjoyment. Fiber crafts today present a world of opportunities for creativity that is far from the fast pace of life. Golden moments spent shaping, stitching, designing, creating, and tying can be among the most rewarding in life. Whereas it is difficult to measure daily progress and rewards in the work world and in family life, fiber crafting offers visible progress, immediate gratification, and personal expression.

Industry has responded to this interest in crafting by developing quality products that increase enjoyment and speed successful results. Fabrics are now available in a broad range of coordinated colors, designs, and textures. A few years ago, for example, a crafter would have been fortunate to locate any fabric close to flesh color; today fabric is available in realistic textures and skin tones for all ethnic groups.

Patterns for sewing by hand or machine are easy to use and available for garments, home decorating, accessories, gifts, and toys. Patterns are also available for quilting, crocheting, tatting, needle arts, embroidery, and more. Many are new patterns; others are updates of earlier winning designs.

Tools include high-tech sewing machines with computer capabilities, conventional machines with improved accessories, sergers, cutting tools, and marking, measuring, and shaping aids.

Notions make crafting fun and easy, and include glue applicators, quick fasteners, liquid fray preventers, easy-threading needles, weights to aid cutting, unique transfer methods, variety threads, and trims. Space age iron-on capabilities make any fabric a fusible. Permanent iron-on film will transfer any crayon or original photo to fabric, which can then be crafted into keepsakes. Glitter, metallic, and jewel-like trims are easy to apply by pressure, hammer, machine sewing, or iron-on techniques.

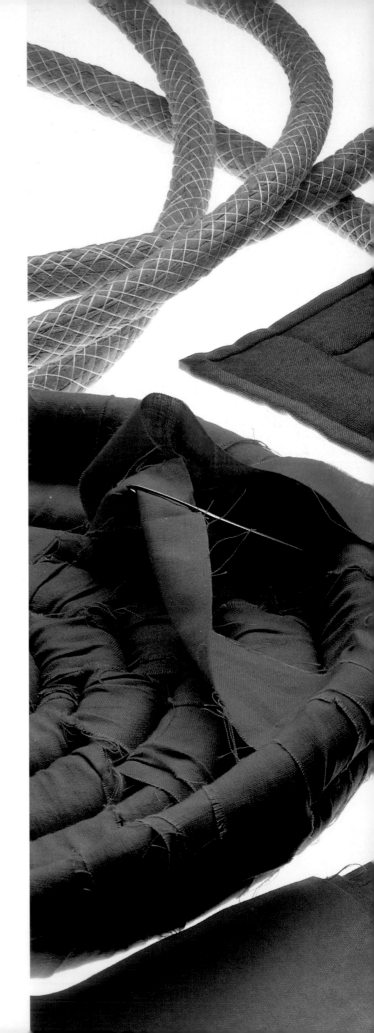

The Rewards of Fiber Art

Everyone can craft — men, women, teenagers, and children. Fiber crafting is flexible. It offers moments precious in solitude or rich with friends. Time schedules are set by the crafter who usually integrates these pleasant moments into a very full life. "I don't have time" is never uttered by crafters who make time for the things they enjoy.

Crafting can be energy producing when used to reduce stress. Working productively with hands clears the mind of concerns. The therapy of crafting is in creating, building, shaping, achieving, and sharing.

Crafting has always given comfort. In nineteenth century New England, mourners remembered loved ones with commemorative embroidered pictures. The purpose of the picture was to give the stitcher legitimate time to mourn for the loved one, and provide a positive task to complete in a reasonable time. Upon completing the project, the stitcher was expected to resume normal living. What a marvelous, positive approach to a reality of life.

The positive effects of handcrafts continue today. Crafting is done by residents of nursing homes, patients in mental health centers, and children in day care centers. Professional people report great benefits from stolen moments that are saved for crafting.

Planning Projects

Planning helps you identify time periods that can be assigned to crafting. Recognize that it is advantageous to work on several projects at a time. Plan a short-term project to run simultaneously with a long-term one. Sort projects by degree of difficulty. Swift gratification comes with the short-term project and encourages the crafter through the long-term project.

Another approach is to work on a portable project simultaneously with a nonportable one. Portable work can be done anywhere, in limited space, with limited tools.

The perfect fabric, stitch, idea, or threads can surface at unlikely times, and you will want to be receptive. Shop at local fabric and craft retailers. Study catalogs for ideas and supplies. While on vacation, visit other fabric and craft stores to add interest to the miles and ideas to your projects. When you are relaxed, you are creative and receptive to ideas.

Make Time Work for You: Organize

Keep a craft shopping notebook in your purse or with your calendar. Include project ideas as well as swatches for matching or coordinating.

Wash, label, and date fabrics and trims when possible; include amount, source, fiber, and intent of purchase, that is, the project you are planning.

Store all the craft materials for each project in one labeled bag.

Large attractive storage boxes for general supplies or individual projects are available at reasonable prices. Select strong boxes of similar size that stack. Label all boxes with a list of the contents.

Store patterns by category.

File carts on wheels are helpful to hold supplies.

Make up a handy kit for portable projects; keep it by the phone, near the door, in the car, or in your briefcase.

Sort craft magazines by project, title, or technique. To add to your collection, review magazines at your library or newsstand, and subscribe to those you enjoy.

Resources for Fiber Art

Craft and fabric retailers who keep up to date with what is new in crafts through trade shows.

4-H organizations, Homemakers Clubs, Extension Service.

County and state fairs.

American Sewing Guild, quilting guilds, and other guilds specific to needlework techniques.

Public schools, public and private colleges, continuing education programs.

Library books, magazines, videos, and films.

Craft catalogs as a source for ideas as well as for products.

Source:

American Sewing Guild. For the chapter nearest you, write to American Sewing Guild, National Headquarters, Box 50936, Indianapolis, IN 46250.

Dorothy Martin is an author, designer, and educator. She identifies crafting as some of her happiest moments wedged between her family and her position as a financial analyst.

Use plastic boxes and notebooks to organize crafts.

Buy Quilting Needles
& Quilting Thread —
Design modules in
order to determine quilt
pattern—

59 for shopping information.

Buy
project
pale pi
color

Color & Design for Quilting

by Charlene Burningham

Quilts are wonderful and satisfying. Not only do they keep us warm physically, but they give us beautiful visual images. It is a satisfying experience to plan, cut, piece, and quilt, but it is even more satisfying to design your own quilt from scratch and choose the best possible colors to interact on the surface of your quilt. I know the reply is probably, "I can't do that" or "I have no training in design and color." I don't buy either of these excuses. Of course, training in color and design helps, but I feel that we all have an inner design sense and that you must learn to rely on your own feelings. Some of our negative thinking comes from early school experiences when lack of drawing skills was confused with lack of design skills. Training in design and color gives one a feeling of confidence in the area as well as greater speed and skill in decision making. This does not mean that lack of training is synonymous with lack of designing skill. We all have an inner sense of balance and placement, but for some it may take more time to make a decision. Rely on yourself; take time for the design pro-

cess to work. At each step of the process, stop and look at your design. Display it where you will walk by it and look at it. You will make your decision after a bit of time.

Definition of Color Terms

Value is the degree of lightness or darkness of a color. Light values are tints, and dark values are shades.

Hue is the name of a color.

Tint is a hue with white added, yielding a color lighter than a pure hue.

Shade is a hue with black added, yielding a color darker than a pure hue.

Tone is a hue with gray added, yielding a color with a gray quality.

Intensity or saturation is the purity or grayness of a color, the relative brightness or dullness. Colors with strong intensity are nearer the pure hue, and colors of weak intensity are approaching a gray.

Complementary colors are colors directly opposite each other on the color wheel. Complementary colors give a strong contrast; when mixed together or placed side by side, they tend to gray each other.

Color

It is impossible to give you step-by-step directions for selecting colors. There are many factors involved in color choices, such as the room in which you are planning to use this quilt, your color preferences, and availability of colors in the shops. You have values laid out in your design, so you need to select fabrics that match those values. Following are some suggestions to help you select colors.

- Limit the value range of the colors selected. Instead of choosing from very light to very dark, you should choose from very light, light, and medium; or from medium through dark.

- Some colors are naturally lighter and brighter, such as yellow, and some are darker, such as purple. This is why yellow is often a difficult color to use unless the intensity is cut back. Purples often read so dark that there is no definition.

- Colors change because of surrounding colors. It is possible to use the same color in several parts of the design and have it read differently because of a phenomenon called simultaneous contrast.

- Using colors with the same intensity helps to unify the quilt; for example, use either all clear, saturated colors or all unsaturated colors, which contain gray.

- The proportion of color used is important. If you really want to use a color that could be a problem because of value or intensity, you should use a small amount of it. By keeping the proportion small, you can usually make the color work.

- When making value judgments, squint at your colors. If one really stands out, it is probably too light, too dark, or too bright.

- When you use prints, the squinting trick also works because you get a blurring and read the fabric as a "visual mix."

A color mock-up of your quilt is helpful. Cut fabric pieces the shape of the design elements, and glue them down on the mock-up. Colored pencils and pens do not give a realistic result. If you like the color placement and interaction, you are ready to start your quilt. If you don't like them, change the colors on the mock-up. Designing the quilt and selecting fabric take time but are essential to the result. Don't start a quilt until you are happy with the design and color.

How to Design a Quilt

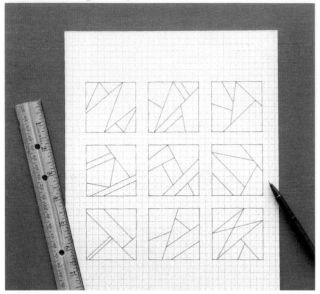

1) Draw a number of 2" or 3" (5 or 7.5 cm) squares on graph paper, with space between each square. Divide each square into six or eight areas.

2) Choose one or two of these designs to do a value study. It is too early to add color, as this introduces another element, so do your value studies using a black pen. You will have black and white as the strongest values, and by drawing lines (fine or heavy, close together or farther apart, and cross-hatching), you will get values of black, white, and gray.

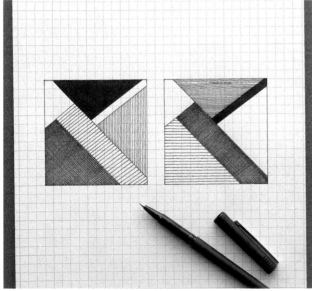

3) Do two or three value studies of the same design. The proportions of black, white, and gray change when the positions are rotated. The designs will look very different if black is placed in the largest shape and, on the next design, in the smallest shape. If the largest shape is solid black, it may overpower the design, especially at the next step in the designing process when the blocks are put together. From these value studies, choose one to work with.

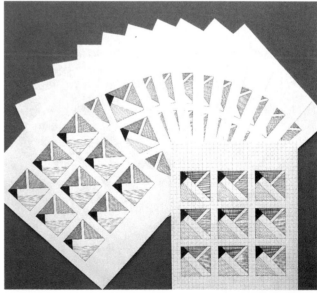

4) Draw a page of the design you chose, take it to a photocopying machine, and copy it several times. Cut the designs apart, and you will then have materials to work with for the next step of the design process. The copies will save a lot of drawing time and free up the design process. A word of warning: the reproduction process distorts the image. Therefore, use the copy as a designing tool, but when making your templates, go back to the original drawing.

How to Rotate Blocks

Block Rotations

Now comes the fun. I find rotating the blocks addictive and always add one more "I wonder what it would look like if I did this." Until now the quilt block has been a single unit. We are now going to work in four-block units. Start by labeling one module as follows: A is the upper left corner, B is the upper right corner, C is the lower right corner, and D is the lower left corner.

After you have gone through the following steps, decide which block you like best and what size you want to make the block. Both the mirror image and the counterclockwise rotations work best with more divisions to the block.

Charlene Burningham is a fiber artist and educator. She is an assistant professor at the University of Minnesota, Department of Design, Housing, and Apparel. Her works have been exhibited nationally in one-woman and husband/wife shows.

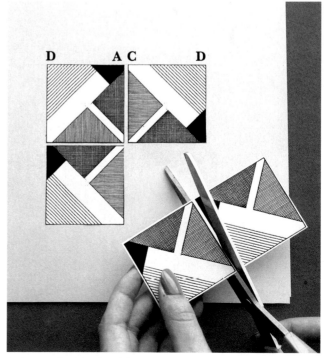

1) Put the first four modules together the same way. The quilt top would then be formed with the units always in the same direction, with AB at the top.

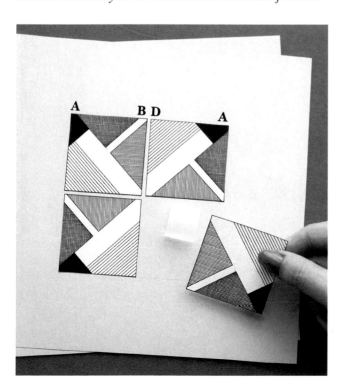

2) Start with AB at the top of the upper left module, and rotate the next module a quarter turn clockwise. DA is now at the top of the upper right module. Continue by rotating each module a quarter turn.

3) Start the block with DA at the top, and continue quarter rotations as in step 2.

(Continued on next page)

How to Rotate Blocks (continued)

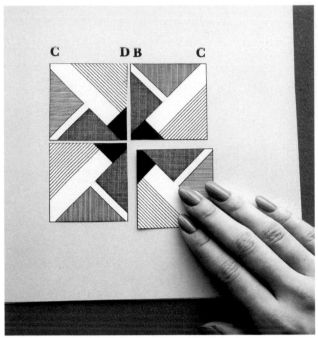

4) Start the block with CD at the top, and continue quarter rotations as in step 2.

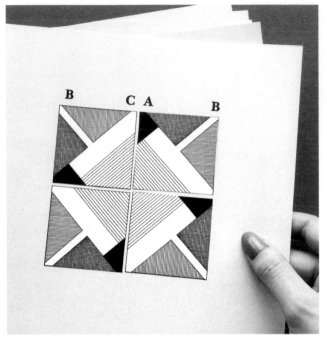

5) Start the block with BC at the top, and continue quarter rotations as in step 2. You now have five new versions of your quilt block. Your block is a four-block unit instead of a single unit. It also looks very different from the single module.

6) Form a reverse image by putting a mirror on the edge of your design. To draw this reversal, turn your original drawing face down, and take it to a light table or window. With the light coming through the paper, trace the design.

7) Make a counterclockwise rotation if you wish to create another design variation. Follow the instructions for clockwise rotations, except rotate the modules counterclockwise.

Find a Rainbow in Your Mailbox

by Peggy Bendel

The following sources make it easy to find the colors you need for a quilt. Each company offers an extensive selection of commercially precolored solid fabrics by mail. All fabrics are the standard quilting type: finely woven, 44/45" (115 cm) wide, and unless noted otherwise, 100 percent cotton. Whether you are searching for a sequence of blending pastels, a balanced set of brights, or a palette of authentic folk art tones, you can surely find them among the hundreds of fabrics currently available.

Cabin Fever Calicoes. Box 550106, Atlanta, GA 30355. Offers an assortment of broadcloth, fine oxford cloth, and lightweight chintz gathered from various manufacturers. Send $2 for 200 swatches.

Keepsake Quilting. Dept. SS1, Dover St., Box 1459, Meredith, NH 03253. Also collects fabrics from different sources, but the weaves, weights, and finishes assembled are quite consistent. Send $2 for 150 swatches.

Quilts & Other Comforts. Box 394, Wheatridge, CO 80034. Has designed a unique line of grayed pastels, which together form a color wheel. Each tint contains some of the color next to it on the wheel for perfect compatibility, and comes in four shades from light to dark. Send $2 for 48 swatches.

Seminole Sampler. Savage Mill, Box 2001, Savage, MD 20763. Offers a dozen colors of polished apple moire, a polyester/cotton blend useful in picture quilts to suggest water or sky, in addition to a wide range of plain solid cottons. Send $3 for 200 swatches.

Peggy Bendel has written seven books and more than 300 magazines articles on sewing-related topics. She is a contributing editor of Sew News.

Heirloom Sewing

by Nancy Zieman

Creation of an heirloom to be treasured for generations in your family can now be done with French hand sewing by machine. Intricate stitchery combined with delicate laces yields exquisite projects in hours instead of days.

Historically, only the wealthy could afford handmade laces. Then, invention of a lacemaking machine made laces affordable around the world. Efforts by the English government to restrict this trade through taxes was thwarted by several enterprising men who risked decapitation to smuggle machines into Calais, France, which is still the home of quality laces.

Today we combine laces and French hand sewing to produce wedding gowns or christening dresses. Other possibilities include detachable collars, decorative yokes, and fancy pinafores.

There are several types of laces and trims made specifically for French hand sewing. Insertion lace has two straight finished sides. Beading lace has evenly spaced openings to allow for ribbon insertion. Edging laces are made with a shaped edge on one side and a straight edge on the other side. Combinations of these laces may be made by the sewer or purchased already joined together. Entredeux, from the French "a space between," is a trim that is made with seam allowances to allow for easy application. Entredeux trim is available in several widths, and is usually white or cream.

Purchase laces and trims by mail or in specialty shops. Select lightweight fabrics such as batiste, organdy, and voile, in cotton or blends in white, ecru, or pastels; fine thread and needles work best. Starch and press all fabrics and trims except puffing strips. As you sew, check periodically to make sure your needles are sharp and unblemished.

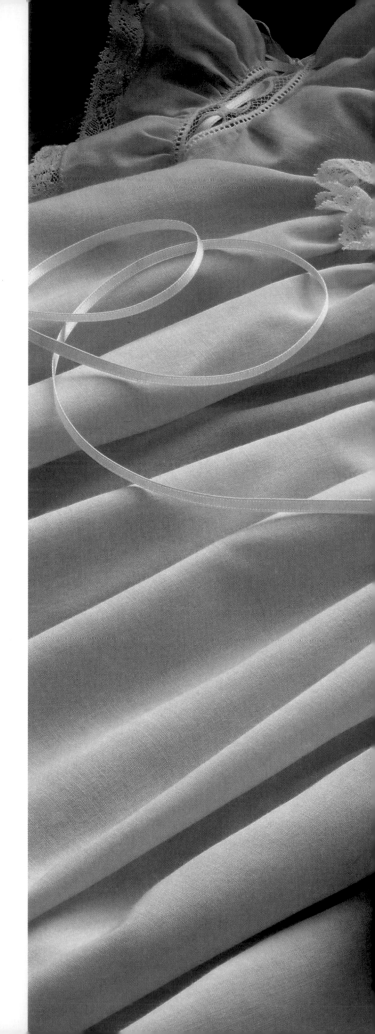

1) **Ribbon twists** add dimension to heirloom sewing projects, using ⅛" (3 mm) wide satin ribbon and decorative sewing machine stitches. Mark vertical lines on fabric and crossmarks at 2" to 3" (5 to 7.5 cm) intervals. At top crossmark, sew ribbon to fabric with a single decorative stitch pattern. Gently twist ribbon 180°, and secure again at next crossmark.

2) **Decorative openings** are created by winged needles, which have extensions on the sides. Stitch with machine embroidery thread and straight, zigzag, or decorative stitches. Sew on fabric that has been pressed extra crisp with several applications of spray starch.

3) **Pin tucks** are created with a pin-tuck foot and twin needles on any zigzag machine. Mark rows with a fabric marker. Attach pin-tuck foot, and stitch the first tuck. Grooves on the bottom of the foot channel fabric as you stitch the remaining tucks.

4) **Entredeux,** a connecting trim, bridges fabrics or laces. Place entredeux and fabric right sides together, raw edges even. With entredeux on top, stitch in the groove. Cut ¼" (6 mm) seam allowances, and finger press them away from the trim. From the right side, zigzag to secure, with a zig in the fabric and a zag in the opening.

5) **Puffing strips** are made with fabric cut 1" to 2" (2.5 to 5 cm) wide and at least twice as long as the desired finished length. Gather both edges, by using two rows of straight stitching or by zigzagging over pearl cotton thread. Pin the strip to your ironing board, and adjust gathers. Steam (don't press), and let it dry. On a serger, stitch both sides without stopping. Place pearl cotton thread between the needle and the upper blade, leaving a tail behind your presser foot. Serge one side, continue with a chainstitch

off the fabric, and serge the remaining side. Gather by pulling on both ends of the pearl cotton thread. Then pin, steam, and let dry.

6) Edging lace is an ideal finish for cuffs and hemlines. Place lace and fabric right sides together, extending fabric ⅛" (3 mm) beyond the straight edge of the lace. Stitch with a small zigzag, encasing extra fabric in your seam. When using a serger, prepare for a rolled hem with a short stitch length. Serge fabric and laces, right sides together. Open and press the seam flat.

7) Insertion lace can be alternated with ribbons or other laces; butt straight edges, and zigzag, placing a zig in one strip and a zag in the other. On a serger, flatlock laces, wrong sides together, guiding them ⅛" (3 mm) to the left of the blade. After stitching, pull the seam flat. For cutwork, place the lace on top of the fabric, and attach with a small zigzag. Turn the piece over, and carefully trim away the fabric.

Sources:
Trims and patterns: *Sandy Hunter, Inc.*, Box 639, Little River Rd., Flat Rock, NC 28731. Pin-tuck foot: *Nancy's Notions®*, Box 683, Beaver Dam, WI 53916. Laces, trims, fabric, and patterns: *Martha Pullen Co., Inc.*, 518 Madison St., Huntsville, AL 35801.

Nancy Zieman is producer and hostess of television's "Sewing with Nancy." She is also president of Nancy's Notions, a sewing mail-order catalog.

Rag Baskets

by Marlys M. Riedesel

Every crafter and sewer I know has a stockpile of fabric, either hidden away or neatly displayed in color families. Each piece once inspired the person to heights of creativity but now just gathers dust. Making rag baskets is a way to use many of those fabrics.

Try a basket in just one smashing fabric, or use a variety of fabrics. When choosing several fabrics, look for a mix of large and small florals, geometrics, stripes, checks, plaids, or tone-on-tone prints.

Anyone can get involved in making baskets. I have taught classes with students from nine to seventy years old. All ages were equally successful.

Use your imagination in embellishing the baskets. Try large wooden or ceramic beads for handles. Wooden handles can be purchased and painted in coordinating colors. You can decorate your basket with woodland figures or silk flowers. Try a sprig of artificial holly for a Christmas basket. Heart-shaped or rectangular wooden bases, available in craft stores, will give your basket a different shape.

Use rag baskets as containers for mail, magazines, and photos; craft projects, knitting yarn, and sewing supplies; jewelry; plants, silk flowers, and baby's breath; fruit, casseroles, and gift-wrapped cookies; guest towels and soap; nursery items such as swabs, oil, and powder. Construct flat coils for coasters, trivets, placemats, and rugs.

Marlys Riedesel is a freelance home economist with experience in retail merchandising and in quilting as well as most other fiber arts.

Supplies
Basket cording or clothesline, ¼" (6 mm) diameter or less.
1" (2.5 cm) strips of lightweight cottons or blends.
Zigzag sewing machine with size 16 (100) needle.
Thread to match fabric.
Rotary cutter or scissors, and ruler.

How to Make Machine-constructed Baskets

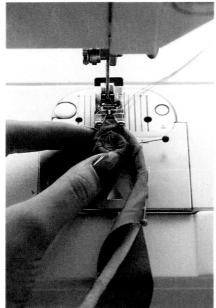  

1) Cover end of cord with fabric strip, and wrap 5" to 6" (12.5 to 15 cm). Pin to hold in place. Bend into spiral shape, and zigzag together. For an oval basket or placemats, make your first turn 3" to 4" (7.5 to 10 cm) from the beginning.

2) Continue to turn and zigzag together until base is desired size. Turn work on edge, pressing base against machine to form sides. At the end of a fabric strip, start another; overlap previous strip. Splice cord, page 116, step 3.

3) Continue sewing until basket is the desired height. End by cutting cord and wrapping fabric slightly past end of cord. Stitch end to previous coil.

Supplies

Basket cording available in ¼", ½", or ¾" (6 mm, 1.3 cm, or 2 cm) diameter.

Lightweight cottons or blends cut in crosswise strips, 1" (2.5 cm) for either of narrow cordings; 1½" (3.8 cm) for wider cording.

Size 13 (85) tapestry needle.

Rotary cutter or scissors, ruler, and masking tape.

How to Make Hand-constructed Baskets

1) Taper end of cording with scissors. Thread tapestry needle onto a fabric strip. Take end of strip opposite from needle, and begin wrapping it tightly around cording about 5" (12.5 cm) from end. Wrap almost to end of cording. Bend end of cording to make a loop. Leave a hole in the loop. Wrap over both cords.

2) Start spiraling cord to form a circle. To fasten, insert needle into hole that was left and pull fabric firmly. Repeat. Construction now consists of wrapping the cording independently 2 or 3 times and then fastening to previous coil 2 or 3 times. Needle cannot pierce fabric, so you must find a spot where you can wiggle needle through.

3) Overlap new strip over end of previous strip. To splice cording, taper ends of old and new cords for about 4" (10 cm). Overlap ends; wrap masking tape around the splice. Continue until bottom is desired diameter. Build up sides to desired height by laying cording on top of previous coil.

4) Add handles to last course of basket. Secure cord 3 or 4 times; wrap cord independently 5" to 6" (12.5 to 15 cm). Bend up into handle shape. Secure to previous coil 3 or 4 times. Continue halfway around basket, and make second handle.

5) Finish basket by cutting cord at an angle and wrapping with fabric. Weave end of fabric in and out, and cut off.

Rug Braiding

by Marilyn Tkachenko

Unlike most other crafts, rug braiding is distinctly American with its roots in the New England states. Braiding itself is an ancient art. There are Biblical accounts of braided hair. Braided jewelry and braided straw floor mats are seen in old paintings. There is no evidence, however, of fabric being used for braiding until the late eighteenth century, when the colonists of New England started braiding fabrics to make small floor coverings. Many New Englanders were frugal out of necessity. No usable material was ever discarded; instead, it was saved for projects such as quilts and rugs. Obviously these first rugs were utilitarian rather than decorative. Historians have been unable to find evidence of braided rugs in the American colonies outside of New England. Climate might be one of the reasons. The Southern colonists didn't need the heavy woolen clothing worn in New England, so woolen scraps weren't available.

Today a handmade braided rug is considered a decorative addition to a room. It can be made any size the braider desires, from a small mat to a room-sized rug. A variety of shapes can be braided: oval, round, square, rectangular, and heart, for example. Patterns are often braided into a rug, and color schemes are planned in detail.

Your rug will blend in if you put two or three colors from your room into your rug. Don't make the center a solid dark color; your rug will look like a target or a hole in the floor. Color changes should be made one strip at a time at the eleven o'clock position. A complete color change will take three rounds.

The manufactured braided rug will never equal the handmade rug in durability and beauty. Braiding accessories greatly reduce the time spent creating these beautiful rugs. For example, Braid-Aid™ is a tool used for folding fabric strips.

The beginning braider should start with an oval rug because this shape is the easiest to braid. Although your rug is reversible, it will have two distinct sides. Braid on the top side, and lace on the bottom side. The top side will be more colorful and have a sculptured look. Keep your tension tight and even, and your rug will be durable enough to last for years.

Fabrics

The most durable rugs are made from 100 percent wool. Collect all your fabric before you start your project. Start your search in your own home; old woolen blankets, coats, and suits can be used. I've used woolen scraps left over from sewing projects.

My favorite supply sources are a woolen mill that manufactures blankets and a company that makes women's coats. Both sources are near my home and sell their scraps for under $1 per pound (.45 kg). My cost to make a 2' by 3' (61 by 91.5 cm) rug would be about $6.

The handmade braided wool rugs I've seen for sale range from $8 to $30 per square foot (.093 sq m). The workmanship and quality of the rugs vary greatly. If you purchase your wool reasonably, you can save significantly by making your own rug.

Fabric Preparation

Wash all fabrics with warm water in a mild soap solution. They may be machine washed on gentle cycle and dried at low temperatures to preshrink and soften the fabric for easier braiding.

Cut strips on the straight grain of the fabric to the desired width. The width is determined by the weight of the wool; follow the manufacturer's directions in the Braid-Aid package. The length of the center braid is determined by the planned size of your finished rug. It will be the width subtracted from the length of the rug; for example, a 2' by 3' (61 by 91.5 cm) rug will have a center braid of 1' (30.5 cm). When the center braid is the desired length, work a modified square corner; this puts a sharp turn in the braid.

Care of Your Braided Rug

The weakest part of your rug is the lacing. Treat it gently. Never shake a braided rug. Don't hang the rug; hanging weakens the lacing. To vacuum, use the attachments and follow around, not across, the braids.

To clean, use the same method you use for the rest of your carpeting. Very little water is needed; only the top surface needs to be washed. Professional cleaners who have experience cleaning braided rugs do an excellent job. Check your area for references. If storing your rug, roll and wrap it in a sheet.

Source:
Braid-Aid Company, 466 Washington St., Pembroke, MA 02359; catalog, $3.

Marilyn Tkachenko teaches rug braiding classes for community education and gives demonstrations for a Minneapolis retailer. She has been a state fair winner for several years.

How to Make an Oval Braided Rug

1) Begin the T-start by threading the strips into the Braid-Aids. Join two of the strips with a bias seam. Trim and press open. (Use a bias seam for adding all future strips.)

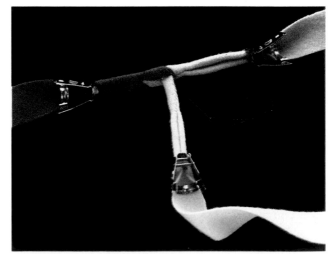

2) Attach the third strip to one side of the seam, with the opening to the right. For the first few inches (centimeters), hand stitching may be necessary to hold folds in place.

3) Braid right strip over center, left strip over center, and continue alternating strips in this order. Keep the opening to the right. Develop an even tension that is tight enough so you can't separate the braids with your fingers. Work to desired length.

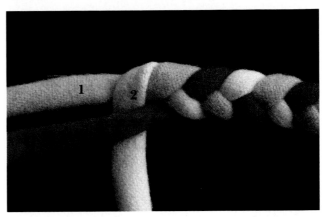

4) Make modified squared corner by numbering the strips from left to right: 1, 2, and 3. Work 1 over 2, 2 over 1, 3 over 2 tightly. Renumber strips from left to right, and repeat once.

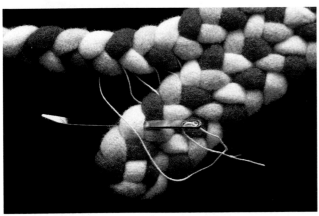

5) Sew two center braids together, starting at first bend and working around T-start; use a sharp needle and linen thread. Switch to bodkin needle. On straight sides, lace every loop of rug and braid. On curved ends, skip loops of braid only.

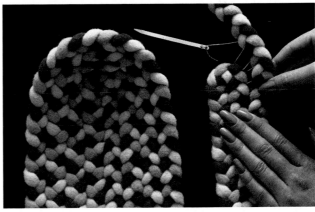

6) Relace if rug cups, skipping more loops of braid. Rippled edge indicates too many skipped loops. On the next round, skip fewer loops, and the problem will correct itself.

7) Finish rug by tapering each strip 5" to 7" (12.5 to 18 cm) on curve. Turn under the edge of each strip, and blindstitch together with matching thread.

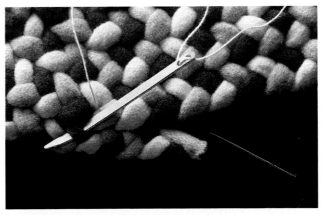

8) Braid to the end. Lace as far as you can, then back-lace several inches (centimeters), and cut the thread. Tuck end into loop, and blindstitch in place.

English Smocking Made Easy

by Betty L. Craig

Smocking is an exciting, versatile craft which has its origin in early folk embroidery and continues to be popular in fashion today. Hundreds of new, inventive smocking stitches allow for countless patterns and endless creativity.

The technique of smocking refers to gathering material into folds and creating designs by stitching through one pleat at a time. It is used on many household items as well as on yokes, bodices, pockets, sleeves, and waistlines of clothing such as nightwear, children's wear, blouses, and dresses.

A decorative pattern results from the use of smocking. In addition, smocking gives shape to the garment. It provides an elasticity that pleats and tucks do not give. Today smocking is used primarily because of its many decorative effects.

For smocking, a lightweight, crisp fabric is best. Suggestions include lightweight polyester and cotton blends, batiste, broadcloth, calicos, or soft flannel.

These materials are suitable because they will gather into pleats. Embroidery floss is used for the decorative stitching. A size 7 or 8 (55 or 60) needle is most often used with three or more strands of floss. (Use a finer thread for batiste.)

Smocking is done before the garment is constructed. The fabric should be preshrunk. The piece to be smocked should be at least three times larger than the finished area, because smocking decreases the size of the fabric.

If a desired commercial pattern does not use smocking, it may be adapted in a pattern with gathers. A basic pattern that involves a small area to be smocked will give best results. When you are working with two identical pieces such as collars, cuffs, or bodice fronts, it is helpful to complete them simultaneously to maintain uniformity.

Before the fabric is smocked, it must be gathered into pleats. A pleating machine may be preferred at this step to accommodate today's busy lifestyle. It provides a fast and efficient way of gathering the fabric. Since buying a pleating machine can be quite costly, one can simply take the fabric to a quilting store and have the piece pleated. The fabric is fed into the machine, which consists of 16, 24, or 32 needles. The

needles are threaded with quilting thread because it is stronger, less likely to tangle, stays in the fabric better, and makes pleats that are fuller and more rounded. The result is evenly pleated fabric that is ready to be smocked. Hint: Before smocking, count the pleats, and mark the center so that symmetrical designs will balance.

The look of the finished pattern will depend on which stitch, or combination of stitches, is selected. A wide variety of stitches may be used. They are completed by working from left to right. Two of them are the cable stitch and the trellis stitch. The cable stitch is used often and is easy to learn. It is a compact stitch with a basket weave appearance. The trellis stitch is versatile and can vary in the number of stitches that compose it. It gives a zigzag effect and can be worked to any height. Two pleats are worked at a time. Stitches are made in a steplike fashion.

The creativity involved with smocking comes into play during the planning of the design. Drawing a sketch of the design on paper before working on the fabric helps to eliminate uncertainty. Choose a dominant color for the theme, and use compatible colors or accent colors suitable for the fabric or design. Using dark, medium, and light colors enhances the design even further.

For Further Reading:

Ellen McCarn on English Smocking, Ellen McCarn. *The Photo Book of Smocking Stitches*, Sandy Hunter.

Betty L. Craig, C.H.E., is owner of Betty Craig & Associates. Her experience includes nine years as a textiles and clothing construction instructor.

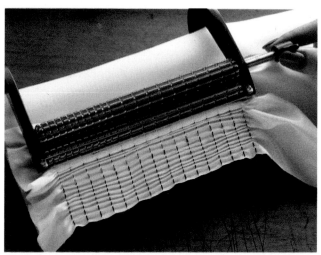

On a pleating machine, fabric is wound on a dowel, and the fabric end is inserted between two rollers. Fabric is fed through by turning a handle at the side of the machine.

How to Make a Cable Stitch

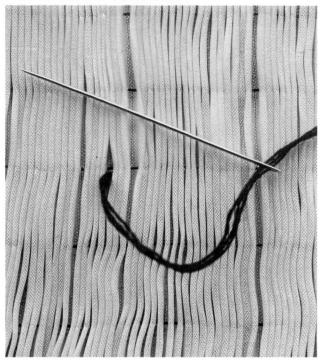

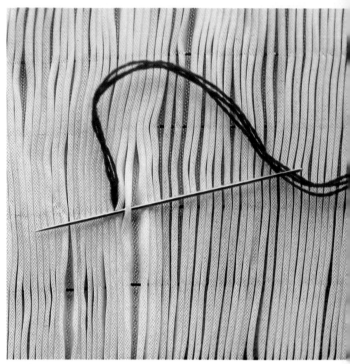

1) Bring the needle through the first pleat from the underside.

2) Place thread above the needle, and stitch under the second pleat.

How to Make a Trellis Stitch

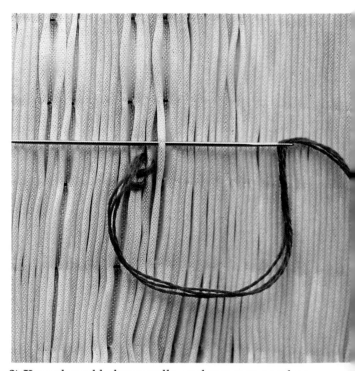

1) Start with bottom cable, bringing the needle through the first pleat from the underside. Placing thread below needle and moving up a quarter of the way between rows 1 and 2, stitch the next pleat.

2) Keep thread below needle, and move up another quarter space to halfway point between rows 1 and 2; stitch the next pleat.

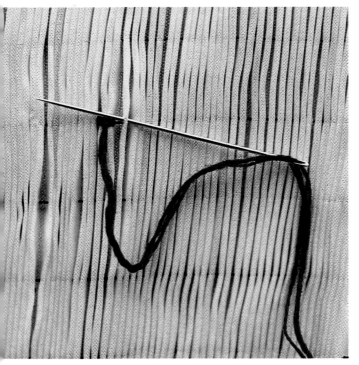

3) Place the thread below the needle, and stitch through the third pleat.

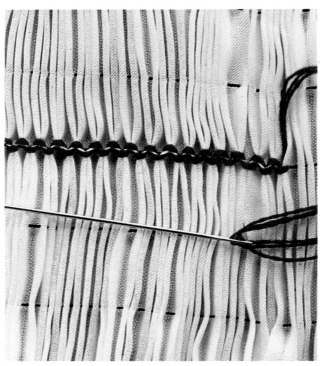

4) Alternate this way until the row is complete. Repeat the procedure for the remaining rows.

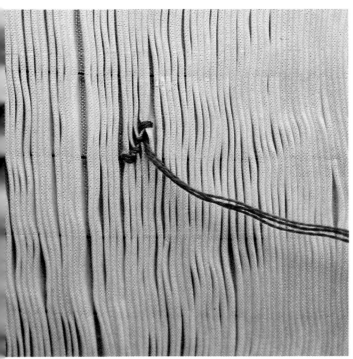

3) Place thread above needle, halfway between rows, and stitch the next pleat, making cable at top of trellis. This stitch completes first half of trellis.

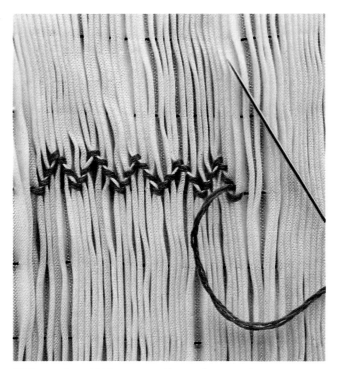

4) Keep thread above needle, and move down a quarter space; stitch next pleat. Repeat. With thread below needle, stitch the next pleat, making cable at bottom of trellis. Repeat steps 1 to 4 as necessary.

Machine Lace Techniques

by Jules & Kaethe Kliot

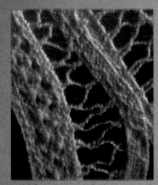

It was man's insatiable desire to adorn himself that led to the development of openwork designs in the fifteenth century. Holes were cut into a woven fabric and then used as the framework for supporting freeform openwork designs that were made with a needle and thread. As the holes were cut larger and larger and the needlework became more elaborate, it became obvious that the base fabric could be done away with entirely and the designs worked "in the air." Thus, the first true lace was conceived and aptly called *punto in aria,* or "points in the air."

Church and royalty's demand for this fabric was so great that, for anyone else, owning or wearing lace was only a dream. Commoners wearing or even possessing lace faced the death penalty. This prevented the general populace from owning it until well into the nineteenth century.

Even without legal restraints, cost alone would put a severe damper on possession of this fabric. When several years of labor might be required to complete a collar, the price at any labor scale would become quite significant. In the world of trade it would not be unusual for a nobleman to trade a vineyard or two for such a magnificent work, to be displayed as a showpiece at the next royal event.

The ingenuity of man, along with the Industrial Revolution of the nineteenth century, enabled the manufacture of lace by machine. This method brought down the cost considerably and for the first time put lace into the hands of the less-than-royal.

The basic techniques for making lace use either a bobbin or needle. The bobbin represents a multi-thread technique. The number of threads could be a dozen or as many as several thousand, depending on the style of the lace. In the alternative technique using a needle, only a single thread forms the lace network. Although machine laces of the nineteenth century closely mimicked the multi-thread bobbin laces, the needle techniques were the ones that were easily picked up by the embroiderers.

The manufacture of needle lace minimized the effort in lacemaking. A narrow woven tape and infillings were used to establish the design. This early lace was called *mezzo punto* and was the direct forerunner of what we now refer to as Battenberg lace. It was not until the latter part of the nineteenth century that this technique gained wide appeal. Initially referred to as Renaissance lace, the name Battenberg was attached to the technique in the early 1890s.

The domestic sewing machine, worked by foot treadle, rapidly gained acceptance by the end of the nineteenth century. As a tool to speed ordinary sewing operations, it soon captured the imagination of the needleworker. Not simply a tool for sewing seams and hems, this machine was to become a speed needle for pure ornamentation. It also permitted longer working hours, eliminating much of the eyestrain that accompanied hand needlework.

By the early twentieth century, the Singer Sewing Machine Company laboratories developed techniques for producing the popular Battenberg laces, even making the tape on the sewing machine. The machine could produce these same designs "in air" without any base fabric. In 1922 Singer printed the first edition of the *Art Embroidery Book*, which was later to expand into the *Art Embroidery and Lace Work Book*.

With the popularity of lace for contemporary adornment, we are on the verge of another revival of lacemaking. The new sophisticated tools and materials at our disposal have reduced the effort. A wide variety of patterns, kits, and specialty tapes are available in the needlework marketplace.

One of the newest materials available is a base material referred to as dissolving stabilizer, a translucent plasticlike material that completely dissolves when wet. Infilling stitches worked directly on this stabilizer rather than in air simplify the process.

The other innovative material is the tape itself. The contemporary tapes are bias woven with a heavy edge thread. Selectively pulling this thread on the inner edge of a curve will cause the tape to contour in a flat and uniform manner.

The procedure for making Battenberg lace on the sewing machine is not difficult, but producing work comparable to that worked by hand requires practice and experimentation. It is by no means an automatic operation. The machine needle again returns to its original role as merely a speed needle. In working patterns and fill stitches, the hand of the worker is the master and skill is required to obtain a uniform and even stitch.

Spending a little time perfecting your technique will be well worth the final reward of making a piece you can be proud of. Experiment by working in an area outside the work, adjusting tension for a balanced stitch. Run the machine at a steady speed, moving the work smoothly and continuously. When you need to stop, stop at a point where the filling joins the tape. To avoid a lot of starting and stopping, make long stitches along the edge of the tape to the next infilling

stitch. Plan your stitch pattern ahead to avoid erratic motions of the work and irregular stitches. If the stabilizer tears when working, use a double layer.

For Further Reading:
Machine Embroidery, McNeill. *Singer Instructions for Art Embroidery and Lace Work,* reprinted by Lacis. *Kalocsai Gephimzes,* Katalin. *Complete Book of Machine Embroidery,* Fanning.

Sources:
Lacis, 2982 Adeline St., Berkeley, CA 94703; catalog, $1. *Nancy's Notions®,* Box 683, Beaver Dam, WI 53916; catalog, free.

Jules and Kaethe Kliot, authors, appraisers, lecturers, and teachers, have been involved with all aspects of lace for over twenty years, gaining recognition as leading experts in this field. They are the owners of Lacis, a supplier of lace-making equipment.

How to Make Battenberg Lace on the Sewing Machine

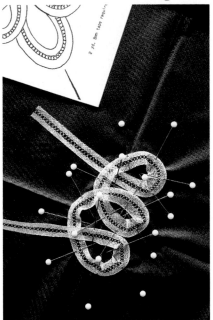

1) Lay the dissolving stabilizer over pattern, and trace pattern onto stabilizer using a nonbleeding pen. Lay the tape on pattern lines, pinning along outer edge of all curves and contouring the tape as necessary.

2) Machine-baste on outer edge of tape, using water-soluble thread and stitching through stabilizer. Where tapes overlap, pull the heavy edge thread on the inner edge of all curves until the tape lies flat.

3) Place a section of stabilizer in 6" (15 cm) embroidery hoop, exposing a section of pattern. Remove presser foot, lower or cover the feed dogs, and reduce thread tension. Set stitch control for straight stitch; lower the presser foot bar.

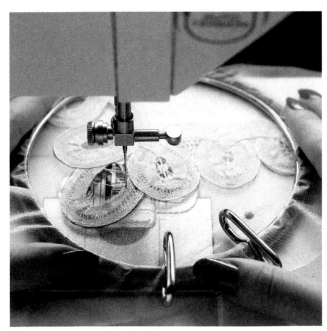

4) Secure thread with 2 to 3 stitches at tape edge. Work infilling pattern in open areas, stitching through stabilizer. To be self-supporting once the stabilizer is dissolved, all lines of infilling stitches must interconnect and join tape edge.

5) Complete all infillings, and cut away stabilizer near outer edge of work. Rinse finished piece in warm water, dissolving any remaining stabilizer. Lay the wet piece on a smooth, flat surface; block by hand, using pattern as guide. Air dry, starch, and press.

Sources

Books

The Book of Smocking, Diana Key

Clothing Care & Repair, More Sewing for the Home, The Perfect Fit, Sewing Activewear, Sewing Essentials, Sewing for the Home, Sewing Specialty Fabrics, Sewing for Style, Timesaving Sewing; Singer Sewing Reference Library®

Complete Book of Machine Embroidery, Robbie Fanning

Creative Serging, Creative Serging Illustrated; Pati Palmer, Gail Brown, and Sue Green

Ellen McCarn on English Smocking, Ellen McCarn

The Fiberworks Source Book, Bobbi A. McRae

French Hand Sewing by Machine, Melissa Stone

Kalocsai Gephimzes, Katalin

Know Your Sewing Machine, Jackie Dodson

Machine Embroidery, McNeill

Overlock Sewing, Coats & Clark

The Photo Book of Smocking Stitches, Sandy Hunter

Power Sewing, Sandra Betzina

The Quilting Primer, Dorothy Frager

Serge a Quilt, Serge & Sew; Ann Person

Sewing with Sergers, Gail Brown and Pati Palmer

Singer Instructions for Art Embroidery and Lace Work, reprinted by Lacis

The Successful Serging Handbook, Leonora Johnson and Sharon Hirschner

Newsletters & Magazines

Aardvark, Box 2449, Livermore, CA 94550

Best Patterns List, The Sewing Workshop, 2010 Balboa St., San Francisco, CA 94121

Creative Needle, Box 99, Lookout Mountain, TN 37350

The Econo-Crafter, RFD 1, Box 5890, Gardiner, MO 04345

G Street Fabrics, 11854 Rockville Pike, Rockville, MD 20852

The Knitting Machine Bookshelf, Box 746, Englewood, NJ 07631

Palmer/Pletsch Update, Suite 269, 2269 Chestnut, San Francisco, CA 94123

Sensational Stitches, Box 1936, Orem, UT 84057

Serger Update, Suite 269, 2269 Chestnut, San Francisco, CA 94123

Sew Beautiful, 518 Madison St., Huntsville, AL 35801

Sew News, Subscription Dept., 1 Fashion Center, Box 3137, Harlan, IA 51537

Sewing Sampler, Box 39, Springfield, MN 56087

The Silver Thimble, 311 Valley Brook Rd., McMurray, PA 15317

Threads, The Taunton Press, Box 355, Newtown, CT 06470

Treadleart Magazine, 25834 Narbonne Ave., Lomita, CA 90717

Catalogs & Fabric Samples

Bee Line Products, Inc., Box 538, Manlieus, NY 13104

Braid-Aid Company, 466 Washington St., Pembroke, MA 02359

Cabin Fever Calicoes, Box 550106, Atlanta, GA 30355

Catherine's of Lexington, Rte. 6, Box 1227, Lexington, NC 27292

Clotilde, Inc., 237 SW 28th St., Ft. Lauderdale, FL 33315

The Fabric Carr, Box 1083, Los Altos, CA 94022

Ghee's, Suite 205, 106 Kings Highway, Shreveport, LA 71104

Herrschners, Inc., Hoover Rd., Stevens Point, WI 54492

JK Originals, 15040 75th Ave. N., Maple Grove, MN 55369

June Tailor, Inc., Box 208, Richfield, WI 53076

Keepsake Quilting, Dept. SS1, Dover St., Box 1459, Meredith, NH 03253

Lacis, 2982 Adeline St., Berkeley, CA 94703

Nancy's Notions®, Box 683, Beaver Dam, WI 53916

The Perfect Notion, 566 Hoyt St., Darien, CT 06820

Porcupine Pincushion, Box 1083, McMurray, PA 15317

Professional Sewing Supplies, Box 14272, Seattle, WA 98114-4272

Quilts & Other Comforts, Box 394, Wheatridge, CO 80034

Quintessence, Box 723554, Atlanta, GA 30339

Seminole Sample, Savage Mill, Box 2001, Savage, MD 20763

Serge & Sew Notions, 14035 38th Place N., Plymouth, MN 55441

Sew Sensational, Box 1936, Orem, UT 84057

Sew Stylish, Box 176, Randleman, NC 27317

Sewing Emporium, 1087 Third Ave., Chula Vista, CA 92010

Speed Stitch, Inc., Box 3471, Port Charlotte, FL 33952

Treadleart, 25834 Narbonne Ave., Lomita, CA 90717

YLI Corporation, 45 West 300 North, Provo, UT 84601

Consumer Information

American Sewing Guild. National Headquarters, Box 50936, Indianapolis, IN 46250. A nonprofit organization of home sewers. Write for address of nearest local chapter.

Thread

Coats & Clark, Suite 351, Patewood Plaza, 30 Patewood Dr., Greenville, SC 29615

DMC Corporation, 107 Trumbull St., Elizabeth, NJ 07206

Streamline Industries, Inc., 234-242 West 39th St., New York, NY 10018

Swiss-Metrosene, Inc., 7780 Quincy St., Willowbrook, IL 60521

Tootal American, Box 1016, Bennettsville, SC 29516-1016

Interfacing

Crown Textile Company, Armo Division, 1412 Broadway, New York, NY 10018

Freudenberg, Pellon Division, 119 West 40th St., New York, NY 10018

Stacy Industries, Inc., 38 Passaic St., Box 395, Wood-Ridge, NJ 07075-0395